床头灯英语学习读本 III

Frankenstein

弗兰肯斯坦

原著　Mary Shelly

　　　[英]　玛丽·雪莱

改编　Andrew Grant

翻译　刘安平　唐树良

主审　李正栓

航空工业出版社

图书在版编目(CIP)数据

床头灯.3:英语学习读本/李正栓等主编.
-北京:航空工业出版社,2004.7
ISBN 7-80183-382-1

Ⅰ.床… Ⅱ.李… Ⅲ.英语-高等学校-水平
考试-自学参考资料 Ⅳ.H310.42

中国版本图书馆 CIP 数据核字(2004)第 051905 号

航空工业出版社出版发行
(北京市安定门外小关东里 14 号 100029)

北京富生印刷厂	全国各地新华书店经销
2004 年 6 月第 1 版	2004 年 6 月第 1 次印刷
开本:787×1092 1/32 印张:75.5	字数:1600 千字
印数:1~8000	(全 10 册)定价:100.00 元

本社图书如有缺页、倒页、脱页、残页等情况,请与本社发行
部联系负责调换。联系电话:64890262 84917422

写在前面的话

——中国人学英语现状分析

◆英语是语言的帝国

全球 60 亿人中,有 8 亿人的母语是英语;2.5 亿人的第二母语是英语。12.3 亿人学习英语,33.6 亿人和英语有关。全世界电视节目的75％、E-mail 的 80％、网络的 85％、软件源代码的 100％使用英语。40～50 年后,全球 50％的人精通英语。全球约 6000 种语言,本世纪末90％将消亡。届时英语作为主导语言的地位将进一步得到提升。

目前中国大约有 3 亿人在学英语,超过英国和美国的人口总和,这是中国努力与时代接轨、与国际接轨的一个重要标志。大量中国人熟练掌握国际通用语言是中华民族走向繁荣富强的必要保障。

◆英语学习的远期目标

在中国英语已经远远超过一个学科的范畴,一个人英语水平的高低总是和事业、前途、地位,甚至命运联系在一起。对于个人来讲,英语在人生旅途中具有战略意义,不失时机地在英语上投入时间、投入精力、投入金钱符合与时俱进的潮流,是明智之举。

◆目前存在的问题

尽管在中国学习英语的人数众多,但收效却令人担忧,学了这么多年英语,能够运用自如的人实在是凤毛麟角。由于运用能力差,无法品尝到英语学习成功的快乐,很多人不得不承认学英语的目的只能是学英语,这就是人们常说的"为了学英语而学英语"。

◆考试的压力对英语学习的积极影响

在我国与个人命运休戚相关的各类考试,如中考、高考、四六级、硕士研究生入学考试、博士研究生入学考试、职称考试、出国考试,都考或只考英语。目前很多人把中国人学不好英语的责任推到英语考试身上,好像中国人学不好英语就是因为有了英语考试,甚至有人还产生了将英语考试废除的想法。

大家可以冷静地反思一下:如果没有各种各样的英语考试,哪里有这么多中国人坚持学英语?国家正是利用了考试这个指挥棒引导很多人去学英语。说句实话,你不能指望每个中国人都怀着与国际接轨的远大抱负去学英语。中国曾经取消过考试,结果造成了人才10年的断层。所以我的看法是在谈论考试的不足时,首先应该承认它在选拔人才、培养人才方面的不可替代的作用。英语考试对中国人学英语起到了很大的积极作用,功不可没。但必须承认:如果真想把英语学好,光会做几道考试题是远远不够的。

◈ **不可缺少的环节**

没有几百万字的输入无法学好英语。语言的习得是一个长期的过程,需要大量的"输入"。一个由汉语武装起来的头脑,没有几百万字英文的输入,即使要达到一般水平也难。绝大多数的英语学习者正是由于缺少了这一环节,所以停留在一个无奈的水平上。

◈ **"圣人"学英语的做法**

在学英语的长远目标和考试的压力共同作用下自然会产生学好英语的强烈愿望,但这一愿望的实现需要有很强的"韧劲"(自我约束力)。春来不是读书天,夏日炎炎正好眠,秋有蚊虫冬又冷,收起书包待明年。随着物质文明的繁荣,总有一些理由使人不能安心学习。这样下去,我们的英语之树永远长不高。古人云:人静而后安,安而能后定,定而能后慧,慧而能后悟,悟而能后得。很有道理。在四川大足佛教石刻艺术中,有一组大型佛雕《牧牛图》,描绘了一个牧童和牛由斗争、对抗到逐渐协调、融合,最后合而为一的故事。佛祖说:"人的心魔难伏,就像牛一样,私心杂念太多太多;修行者就要像牧童,修炼他们,驯服他们,以完美自己的人生。"那些具有很强的心力的人,我们姑且称其为"圣人",他们能够驯服那些影响我们学习的大牛、小牛,抵制各种诱惑,集中精力,专心学习,到达成功的彼岸。

◈凡人的困惑

在目前的教育体系中,学好英语是需要坚忍不拔的毅力的。但问题是我们大多数平凡的人无法和圣人相比,所以在学英语的征途上,失败者多,成功者少。客观地讲,在中国英语学习的失败率应该在99%以上,即使采用不是太高的标准来衡量——原因是英语的门槛太高了。有的人说难道我们不能把所有的或者是大多数的人都变成圣人吗,这样大多数人就可以学好英语了。我们不得不承认大多数凡夫俗子是不能够成为圣人的。值得我们深思的是目前的英语学习体系中没有给大多数人提供一条平坦的道路。

◈兴趣——英语学习成功的真正源泉

我和大家一样都是凡人,我也曾经遇到过学英语的困惑,干巴巴的课文无论怎样都激不起我的兴趣。幸运的是我有一个在国外生活多年的姐姐,有一次她回国,给我带来很多浅显有趣的读物。我拿起一本一读,觉得很简单,一个星期就读完了。就英语学习而言,一部英文小说其实就是用英语建构的一个"虚拟世界"。那里有人,有人的心灵和人与人之间关系的揭示,有人与自然、与社会的冲突和调和。走进一部英文小说,你实际上就已经"生活"在一个"英语世界"里了,不愁没有东西可学。经典作品要读,写得好的当代通俗小说也要读。我一共读了50本,从此对英语产生了兴趣,英语水平有了很大的提高。还是爱因斯坦说得好:"兴趣是最好的老师。"

◈《新概念英语》的主编 L. G. Alexander 的启示

中国人读英语书有个特点,越读不懂越读,习惯于读满篇都是生词的文章。L. G. Alexander 先生是世界著名的英语教学专家,他的经典之作《新概念英语》对于中国的英语教学产生了深远的影响。针对这一现状 Alexander 先生说过,"记住,你的接受型词汇量(即你听或阅读英语时能理解的部分)比你的积极词汇量(即你在说或写时能自如运用的部分)要大得多。如果要扩大词汇量,最好的办法是多听英语,多读英语,但不要超出自己的水平,阅读那些比你目前水平稍低的书。"这才是提高英语运用能力的诀窍。

本套读物特色:

●情节曲折:本书选材的时候非常注意作品的吸引力。比方说:

《查特莱夫人的情人》(Lady Chatterley's Lover):我当年读大学的时候,班上每个同学都买一本看。有的同学甚至熄灯后,打着手电筒躲在被窝里看。

《吸血鬼》(Dracula):这个故事真吓人,我看完以后好几天没睡好觉。后来我的一个学生说他对英语从来不感兴趣,我就把这本小说推荐给他。后来他对我说:"这是我一口气读完的第一本英语书,就是太吓人了。老师,能不能再给我来一本?"

《呼啸山庄》(Wuthering Heights):讲述的是一个骇人听闻的复仇故事,当初没有想到这本书的作者竟然是一个生活在几乎与世隔绝环境中的女孩。

《飘》(Gone With The Wind):几乎所有的美国女孩都读过这本书,主人公斯嘉丽是美国女孩的偶像,可以说我见过的每个美国女孩都是一个 Scarlet.

......

本套丛书中包含的都是在你一生中值得去读的作品,读这些作品不但可以提高你的英语水平,而且能够提高你的个人修养。

●语言地道:本套读物均由美国作家执笔,用流畅的现代英语写成。他们写作功底深厚,这是母语为非英语的作者很难达到的。

●通俗易懂:本书是用 3300 个最常用的英语单词写成,易读懂,对于难词均有注释,而且采用英汉对照的形式。你躺在床上不用翻字典就能顺利地读下去。

●配有高质量的音带:这样大家可以在读懂的基础上进行听的训练,请注意:阅读需要量,听力更需要量。大量的语音输入是用英语深入交谈的源泉。

这套读物供你在下课后或下班后闲暇时阅读,她的优点是帮你实现英语学习的生活化,使英语成为你生活的一部分。这才是英语成功的真谛,更是任何有难度事情成功的真谛。

王若平 于北京

本系列丛书学习指导咨询中心:

北京通向未来语言研究所

地　　址:北京市海淀区清华南路华清商务会馆 1501 室

邮　　编:100083

E－mail:wrx1@vip.sina.com

网　　址:www.sinoexam.com

故事梗概

　　年轻的英国船长罗伯特·沃尔顿率领着他的船员们驾船到冰天雪地的北极地区探险，希望能找到一条穿过北冰洋到达亚洲的航线。由于天气严寒，北冰洋的冰越结越厚，眼看船只就要被坚冰困住。他们突然发现一个人驾着雪橇从冰面上驶向远方，而最令他们震惊的是，那个人的身材——那简直就是一个传说中的巨人。第二天，他们在冰面上又发现了另外一个人。这个人漂在一块浮冰上，拉雪橇的狗已全部死去。此人身体虚弱，看来已多日滴水未进。船长命船员们将他救上船来并进行救助。此人稍稍恢复后，给船长讲述了他的故事：

　　他名叫维克多·弗兰肯斯坦，家住在日内瓦。家庭富裕，口碑极好。为了研究科学并造福于人类，他告别了父亲、弟弟和美丽的未婚妻伊丽莎白到德国去上大学。经过数年的潜心研究，他利用从人的尸体上取下的骨骼和动物的器官造出了一个人———个丑陋无比的庞然大物。他对这个怪物十分害怕，因而将它抛弃。那怪物到处流浪，由于其丑陋无比，人人都把它看成妖怪，无人肯与他做朋友。他救了落水儿童，却被孩子的父亲开枪打伤。激愤之下，他决定要报复弗兰肯斯坦博士，因为他认为是博士将他造出却又弃之不理才造成他在世界上孤独无依的现实。他杀死了博士的弟弟，却嫁祸于女仆人。以今后不再报复为条件，他强迫博士为他造出一个配偶。遭到拒绝后，他杀死了博士的好友亨利，并在博士的新婚之夜杀死了新娘伊丽莎白。为了复仇，博士到处追逐这个怪物，并一直追到了北极。

　　博士知道自己命已不久，他要求沃尔顿船长去杀死那个怪物以免有更多的人被杀。但在临终时，他告诉船长他已宽恕了那个怪物，因为自己没有善待他而使他悲惨孤独地活在世上。最终怪物也因悔恨自己的所作所为而自杀身亡。

目　　录

Chapter One　The Man on the Frozen Sea ················· （2）

第一章　冰海上的人 ···································· （3）

Chapter Two　The Story Begins ····················· （14）

第二章　故事开始了 ·································· （15）

Chapter Three　I Discover a Great Secret ············· （22）

第三章　我发现了一个大秘密 ························ （23）

Chapter Four　The Monster ························· （30）

第四章　怪物 ·· （31）

Chapter Five　One Incredible Night ················· （34）

第五章　一个难以置信的夜晚 ························ （35）

Chapter Six　Madness! ···························· （40）

第六章　疯狂 ·· （41）

Chapter Seven　A Murder Occurs ··················· （52）

第七章　一场凶杀案发生了 ·························· （53）

Chapter Eight　The Figure in the Woods ············· （58）

第八章　林中的身影 ·································· （59）

Chapter Nine　Searching for a Killer ················ （64）

第九章　寻找凶手 ···································· （65）

Chapter Ten　The Second Victim ··················· （70）

第十章　第二个牺牲品 ································ （71）

Chapter Eleven　Face to Face with the Monster ········ （78）

第十一章　直面怪物 ·································· （79）

Chapter Twelve　The Monster Speaks ··············· （86）

第十二章　怪物所讲的故事 ·························· （87）

Chapter Thirteen   A Confession ················· (106)

第十三章 坦白 ··· (107)

Chapter Fourteen   The Promise ················· (114)

第十四章 誓言 ··· (115)

Chapter Fifteen   The Second Monster ········· (120)

第十五章 第二个怪物 ································· (121)

Chapter Sixteen   The Monster's Threat ······· (130)

第十六章 怪物的威胁 ································· (131)

Chapter Seventeen   More Deaths and Sadness ······· (138)

第十七章 更多的死亡与痛苦 ·············· (139)

Chapter Eighteen   In Prison ···················· (148)

第十八章 在狱中 ······································· (149)

Chapter Nineteen   A Joyous Wedding ········· (156)

第十九章 欢快的婚礼 ································· (157)

Chapter Twenty   The Wedding Night ········· (164)

第二十章 新婚之夜 ····································· (165)

Chapter Twenty-one   The Last Fight ········· (172)

第二十一章 最后一战 ································· (173)

Chapter Twenty-two   Peace at Last ··········· (182)

第二十二章 最终的安宁 ···························· (183)

CHAPTER ONE
The Man on the Frozen Sea

It was wintertime, in the middle of the wild, cold lands of the Arctic. In this land, the sea was frozen all year long. The large, floating pieces of ice were slowly freezing together. They could have crushed the small ship that was trying to sail in the waters. Almost all the water in the oceans was frozen.

The ship's young English captain, Robert Walton, stood on the ship's deck and stared out at the frozen sea. He knew that all the men on the ship's lives were in danger. He had taken them here because of his own *desires* — to *explore* lands that had never been seen before. Walton had wanted to find a way through the oceans from Europe to the jewels and silks in Asia. He had believed that traveling through the North Pole's waters could show him the way to Asia. If he found a new path, all of Europe would become rich.

2

第一章
冰海上的人

隆冬季节，北极中部大地既荒凉又寒冷。在这里海洋常年冰封。大块的浮冰正缓缓地冻结在一起，任何试图在这片水域航行的小船都会被撞碎。海洋中的水几乎全部冻结在一起了。

这位年轻的英国船长，罗伯特·沃尔顿，正站在甲板上凝视外面冰封的海面。他很清楚，船上所有的生命都面临着危险。他想去探测以前从未有人见过的地域，正是这个愿望使他将他们带到了这里。沃尔顿一直盼望能穿过大洋，发现一条水道从欧洲直达充满珍宝和丝绸的亚洲。他一直相信他可以穿过北极水域到达亚洲。如果他能发现一条新的航线，整个欧洲都会富裕起来。

desire: *n.* 欲望；愿望 desire for sth./to do sth. 想得到某物/想干某事

explore: *v.* 探索；冒险 explore new solutions to the problem 探索这一问题新的解决方法

3

Walton came from a wealthy family, and he did not have to work. But instead, he had chosen to live a hard life at sea, being an ordinary sailor. He had experienced thirst, cold, hunger, and terrible weather to prepare himself for this great journey.

But now it seemed that the ice would destroy his ship. Walton did not know if any of his men would see their families in England again. In the afternoon, a thick mist that had covered the ship all morning began to disappear. When it did, the men saw something *amazing*. "Look, Captain!" shouted one of the men. He pointed to a dark object near the ship. "It's a sled, sir. And those dogs are pulling it quickly!" Walton ran over to look. "Look at that man on the sled!" he cried. "He is the biggest man I have ever seen. He can't be human! Why is he here, in the middle of a frozen sea, hundreds of miles away from *civilization*?" As the men watched, the strange person had disappeared into the distance. Walton and his crew did not know what to think or say. The next morning when Walton came onto the deck, he saw that his

4

沃尔顿是一个富家子弟，他根本不需要去工作。但是相反，他却选择了艰苦的海上生涯，当了一名普通的水手。为了准备这次伟大的航行，他已经忍受过干渴、寒冷和饥饿，还经历过各种恶劣的天气。

但现在看来，冰层会将他的船毁掉。沃尔顿不知道他手下的人是否还能再次看到远在英国的亲人。下午时分，笼罩了船舶整整一上午的浓雾开始消散。就在这时，水手们发现了一件令人惊讶的事。"船长，快看！"一位水手指着船附近的一个黑色物体喊道，"先生，是一架雪橇，那些狗正飞快地拖着它跑！"沃尔顿立刻跑过去看，"快看雪橇上那个人！"他高喊，"他是我所见过的体形最大的人，他不可能是个人！他为什么会到这冰封的海面上，一个离文明社会几百英里远的地方来呢？"就在水手们观望时，那个怪人已消失在远方。沃尔顿和船员们简直不知该做何说，甚至不知该做何想。第二天清晨，沃尔顿来到甲板上，他发现水手们正和船舷下方冰面上的某个人说话。他来到水手们中间，发现一块大浮冰上停着一架雪橇，而浮冰正缓缓地向船只靠拢。冰上载着一架雪橇、几条狗和一个人。狗已全部死去，但人还活着。他正用一块木板缓缓地向船只划过来。"又是一个单独呆在冰上的人！到底发生了什么事？但这个人不是我们昨天所见到的那个巨人。"沃尔顿对众人说。

amazing: adj. 使惊奇；使惊讶

civilization: n. 文明；开化

men were talking to someone on the ice below them. When he joined his men, he saw a sled sitting on a large piece of ice. The ice was slowly coming towards the ship. On the ice were a sled, some dogs and a man. All the dogs were dead, but the man was alive. Slowly, he moved himself towards them, using a piece of wood. "Another man alone on the ice! What is happening? But this isn't the *enormous* person we saw yesterday," Walton said to his men.

"Hello, sir! Here is our captain," said one of the sailors to the man below. "Can we help you? Will you come onto our ship?"

"You look almost dead, friend!" said Walton. "Let us help you." "Thank you, sir," answered the man in a weak voice, "but first, I must know where you are going." Walton did not understand why a man who was almost dead would ask these questions, when his life was *in danger*. But he said, "We're exploring the North Pole, sir." The strange man smiled and said to himself, "North is good." Then, he let Walton's men help him up to the ship.

"先生，您好！这位是我们的船长。"一位水手对下面的人说，"我们能帮助您吗？您愿意上我们的船吗？"

"您看来快要死了，朋友！"沃尔顿道，"请让我们来帮助您。""谢谢您，先生，"那个人用微弱的声音说，"但首先我要知道您要到哪儿去。"沃尔顿难以理解一个生命垂危的人居然还会问这样的问题。但他还是说，"先生，我们正要到北极去探险。"陌生人微微一笑，自言自语道，"北极不错。"然后他才让沃尔顿的人将他扶上了船。那个人上船后，船上的医生告诉沃尔顿那人的双腿几乎已冻坏，而且身体极度瘦弱，他可能已有很多天没吃过东西了。"给他裹上几条毯子，把他放在火炉边上，"沃尔顿吩咐。"等他暖和过来后，让

enormous: adj. 巨大的
an enormous amount of money一笔巨款
in danger: 处于危险之中

Frankenstein

When the man was on the ship, the ship's doctor told Walton that the man's legs were almost frozen, and his body was extremely thin. Probably, he had not eaten for many days. "Give him some blankets, and put him near the fire," said Walton. "Then when he is warm, give him some soup and put him in my room. He can sleep there. When he is better I will talk to him."

But for two days the man could not speak. Walton was afraid the man was *insane*, because of the wild look in his eyes. Often, his face looked terribly frightened by something. But there were many moments when the man's eyes showed kindness. Walton knew he was glad to have a little care in this wild land.

Finally the man was strong enough to talk. Walton sat down in a chair and asked him, "Friend, what are you doing alone, out on the *dangerous* ice?" In a weak voice the man said, "I'm looking for someone who is in a sled like mine." "The day before we found you, we saw a strange, enormous person in a sled. Is that the man you

8

他喝点热汤，并把他送到我的舱室里来，他可以睡在我那儿。等他好一些后，我有话要对他说。"

但两天过去了，那个人还是不能说话。沃尔顿看到那个人眼中那狂乱的神色时，怀疑他已精神错乱。那个人经常会露出对某些东西极为害怕的神情，但也有很多时候他的目光中透着善良。沃尔顿明白那是因为他在这片荒凉之地得到了这些关怀而高兴。

那人的身体状况渐渐好转，终于能开口说话。沃尔顿坐在一张椅子上问他，"朋友，你孤身一人到这危险的冰面上来干什么？"那人用微弱的声音答道，"我在寻找一个乘雪橇的人，他的雪橇和我的相似。""我们在看到你的前一天，曾看到过一个奇怪的巨人乘坐着一架雪橇。他就是你要找的人吗？"沃尔顿问道。陌生人睁大了眼睛，并试图从床上爬起来。"是的，"他高声说，"那怪物走的是哪条路？

insane: *adj.* 疯狂的；精神失常的 an insane person / policy 一个疯子 / 一项疯狂的政策
dangerous: *adj.* 具有危险性的

want to find?" asked Walton. The stranger's eyes became very large. He tried to climb out of the bed. "Yes!" he cried. "Which way did the monster go? How many dogs did he have? How much food! I have to find him!" However, the man was so weak that he immediately fell back on-to the bed in pain. "Stay calm!" said Walton. "You are still very sick, and you should not be-come upset." "You are right," said the stranger. "You have saved my life. You probably want to know why I am here, and who that other person is. The story is so terrible that I cannot talk about it now. But perhaps, I shall tell you the truth soon. I must tell someone this terrible secret before I die..." After some days the man got better and was able to walk again. He *spent* his time looking for the mysterious sled, but he also listened to Walton talk about his dreams of finding a sea path to Asia and exploring the world. One day when they were on the deck, Walton said, "Friend, I would give up my money and even my life in the search for knowledge. If Europe becomes strong because of

他还有几条狗？有多少食物？我必须找到他。"但是那人太虚弱了，立刻他又痛苦地倒回到床上。"不要激动！"沃尔顿说道。"你病得很重，不应该着急。""你说的对。"陌生人说。"你曾救过我的命，你很可能想知道我为什么会到这儿来，以及那个人到底是谁。但这个故事太可怕了，我现在无法对你讲。不过，也许我很快把会把真相告诉你。在我死去之前，我必须把这个可怕的秘密告诉某个人……"几天后，那个人的身体又好了一些，可以下床走路了。他把所有的时间都用来寻找那架神秘的雪橇，但他也听沃尔顿谈论自己的梦想，即要找到一条通往亚洲的新航线并探索这个世界。一天，当他们在甲板上时，沃尔顿说，"朋友，为了寻求知识，我愿放弃我的金钱，甚至是我的生命。如果我的航行使欧洲富强了，那么就是以我个人的生命为代价，这也是值得的。"陌生人两眼盯着沃尔顿，"请你千万不要这样想。如果这样想，你只会过一种悲惨的生活。"他说，"我把我的故事讲给你听，你就会明白我曾经像你一样，怎么样用我的一生来寻求知识。我当时坚信我是通过研究科学来为人类造福。但我却只给所有我深爱的人带来了悲伤和死亡，而且我自己也很快就要死了。请听我讲一讲我的遭遇吧，不要让这种事再发生在你的身上。"沃尔顿不知当做何想，"我的朋友，如果你肯对我讲出你的遭遇，也许我可以帮助你呢。"那个人几乎要笑出来，"没有人能帮助我。我感激您的美意，但现在什么也改变不

spend: v. 花费（时间、金钱等）

11

my travels, my life would be a small price to pay! " The stranger stared at Walton. " Don't think this way. You'll only have a life of *misery* if you do," he said. "I will tell you my story, and you will see how I spent all my life looking for knowledge, like you. I believed I was helping human beings through the study of science. But I only brought misery and death to everyone I loved, and I will die soon myself. Listen to my story, and don't let this happen to you." Walton did not know what to think. "Perhaps if you tell me your story, I can help you, my friend." The man almost laughed. "No one can help me. I thank you for your great kindness, but nothing can change my future now. I must do one more thing while I am alive. Then I will be happy to die and leave this terrible life." The two men went to Walton's room, and the man began his story.

了我的未来了。我必须趁活着时再做一件事，然后我会幸福地死去，远离这种可怕的生活。"
两人来到沃尔顿的舱房，那人开始讲他的故事。

misery: *n.* 悲惨；不幸；痛苦
the misery of toothache 牙疼
的痛苦

13

CHAPTER TWO
The Story Begins

I am Victor Frankenstein. For many years, my family was one of the most respected in the city of Geneva, Switzerland. My life as a child was very happy. My parents treated me and my two young brothers, William and Ernest, with great care and love. One year, my father met a noble Italian couple named Lavenza, and became friends with them. When the Lavenzas died, he decided that our family would care for their daughter, Elizabeth Lavenza. Soon young Elizabeth came to Geneva to live with our happy family. Elizabeth was a year younger than I. Although we called her my cousin, Elizabeth was like a sister to me. We spent many happy hours together when we were young. Elizabeth loved to explore the mountains and lakes near Geneva. She loved nature, and did not ask questions about it. But I *was interested in* science: studying why things happened in nature. I felt that

14

第二章
故事开始了

我叫维克多·弗兰肯斯坦。多年以来，我家一直是瑞士日内瓦城中最受人尊敬的家庭之一。我的童年非常幸福。我的父母对我和我的两个弟弟——威廉和厄内斯特——予以无微不至的关心和爱护。有一年，我的父亲结识了一对姓拉凡萨的高贵的意大利夫妇，并和他们结成了好友。拉凡萨夫妇死后，父亲决定由我们家来照顾他们的女儿——伊丽莎白·拉凡萨。很快小伊丽莎白来到了日内瓦，并住进了我们这个幸福的家中。她比我小一岁，我虽然称她为表妹，但她就像是我的亲妹妹一般。我们少年时在一起度过了无数美好的时光。伊丽莎白喜欢到日内瓦附近的群山和湖泊中去探险。她热爱大自然，但从不问和大自然有关的问题。而我却对科学感兴趣，喜欢研究为什么这些事情会在自然界发生。我感到大地和天空中隐藏着我不知晓的重大而奇妙的秘密，而且我想发现它们。我少年时有一个世界上最好的朋友，他的名字叫亨利·克勒瓦尔。我觉得他会终生做我的朋友。亨利是一个快乐的少年，喜欢写勇士故事，而我总是津津有味地去听这些冒险故事。没错，我的童年实在太幸福了！但它太美好了，因此不能永远持续下去。我有慈爱的父母、一个亲爱的妹妹兼朋友、两个快乐的弟

be interested in: 对某物有兴趣 [搭配] be interested in sth.

the earth and sky hid great and wonderful secrets from me, and I wanted to discover them. When I was young my best friend in the world was a boy named Henry Clerval. I felt that he would be my friend for life. Henry was a happy boy who enjoyed writing stories of brave soldiers. I always enjoyed listening to these adventures. Yes, what a happy childhood I had! It was too good to last forever. I had kind parents, a dear sister and friend, two happy little brothers, and the best friend in the world, Henry. I had everything in life... and then I destroyed it all! You see, Walton, my interest in science was too strong. I decided to find out the greatest secrets of nature. No one had ever studied these things before. But when I was thirteen years old, my only interest in science was very good. I wanted to find a way to *cure* sicknesses forever. I only wanted to help people, and stop them from dying. These childhood dreams of mine were so good and brave!

When I was fifteen, something happened that made me become even more interested in the world

弟和一个世上最好的朋友亨利。生活中的一切东西我都有了……后来我又把这一切都给毁了！你要明白，沃尔顿，我对科学的兴趣实在是太强烈了，因此我决定要发现自然界中那些最大的秘密，而以前从未有人研究过这些东西。但当我十三岁时，我对科学的惟一兴趣是出于非常善良的动机——我想找出一个永久治愈疾病的方法。我只是想帮助人们，让他们不会死去。我这些童年时的梦想实在是太美好，太大胆了！

我十五岁那年发生了一件事，它使我对自然界的兴趣更加浓厚。当时日内瓦遭遇一场暴

cure: v. 治愈 cure sb. of sth. 治好某人的病

17

of nature. There was a terrible storm in Geneva, and suddenly *lightning* hit an old tree near our house. In moments, the tree was on fire, and after an hour there were only small pieces of wood on the ground. I had never before seen anything destroyed so quickly. That night, I began to think about the amazing powers of electricity. As the years went by, I began to *wonder* if there were other, even more amazing ways I could use electricity. When I was seventeen years old, I was getting ready to leave my home in Geneva to go to college. I was going to study at the University of Ingolstadt, a small school in Germany. All my ideas about electricity, nature, and science were still in my head. I was excited to learn more about them all. But then, the first tragedy of my life happened. Elizabeth had become seriously sick with a fever, and her life was in danger. My mother wanted to care for Elizabeth herself, although we told her it was not safe to do this. Within a few days, my mother also had the fever, and on the fourth day she was almost dead. As she lay in her bed, she

风雨，闪电突然击中了我家附近的一棵老树。它迅速起火，一小时后地上已是剩的几块木片，在这以前我还从未见过有什么东西被毁灭得如此迅速。那天晚上我开始思考电的惊人能量。随着年岁的增长，我开始思索是否还有其他更惊人的用电方式。我十七岁时，就已做好准备，要离开家乡日内瓦，到德国一所不大的学校——英格尔斯塔特大学去学习。当时我所有关于电、自然和科学的想法仍深印在我的脑海中，而且能掌握更多这些方面的知识使我感到兴奋。但就在那时，我生命中的第一场悲剧发生了，伊丽莎白染上了极严重的热病，生命垂危。我母亲想亲自照顾伊丽莎白，尽管我们都告诉她这样做不安全。几天时间里母亲也染上了热病，第四天她就生命垂危了。她躺在床上，把伊丽莎白的手放在我的手中说，"伊丽莎白，维克多，好好照顾你们的父亲和弟弟们。如果我知道你们俩将来会结婚，我死也瞑目了。答应我吧。"我和伊丽莎白对视了一眼，我就在母亲面前保证要娶她为妻。母亲死后，我不愿意离开家，但几星期后父亲对我说我该走了。亨利也来向我告别，而要离开他则让我很难过。他想和我一起去上大学，但他父亲不允许，因为他想让儿子留在日内瓦和他一起做生意。

lightning: *n.* 闪电 [谚语] lightning never strikes in the same place for twice. 相同的事不会再次发生。 lightning-bug: *n.* 萤火虫

wonder: *v.* 想知道 wonder about sth. 想知道某事；对某事好奇。如：I wonder about his identity. 我想知道他的身份。

asked all the family to come to her. She placed Elizabeth's hand in mine and said, "Elizabeth and Victor, take care of your father and your brothers. I can die peacefully if I know that one day you two will get married. Promise me this." Elizabeth and I looked at each other, and I promised to marry her in front of my mother. After my mother died, I didn't want to leave my family, but after a few weeks my father told me that I should go. Henry came to say goodbye to me. I was very sad to leave him. He wanted to go to college with me, but his father wouldn't *allow* it. He wanted Henry to stay in Geneva, and join his business.

As I told Henry and my family goodbye, I knew that for the first time in my life, I was going out to see the world — alone.

CHAPTER THREE
I Discover A Great Secret

我向家里的亲人和亨利道别时，我就明白我有生以来第一次要孤身一人去闯世界了。

allow: v. 允许；许可

CHAPTER THREE
I Discover a Great Secret

At the university, I immediately began to study science. I still wanted to find ways to cure sicknesses, and make human lives better, just as I had when I was a boy. Professor Waldman, my favorite teacher, told me that I should study both modern and ancient science. "If you use your *understanding* of both kinds of science," he said, "you can discover many things. You will understand how the human body works."

"You are right, Professor," I said. "But I want to know more."

In that moment, I realized that I wanted to learn the great secrets of how the human body was created!

Professor Waldman saw how excited I was, but he did not know what I really wanted to do. He told me, "Victor, I am happy with your ideas, and I believe that you will become a great scientist. I will

第三章
我发现了一个大秘密

在大学里，我立即开始研究科学。就像我少年时代希望的那样，我仍想找到治愈疾病的方法，让人类生活得更美好。我最喜爱的老师——沃尔德曼教授告诉我应该既研究现代科学，也研究古代科学。"如果你能把对这两种科学的理解作为基础，"他说，"你会发现许多东西。你会掌握人体的运行原理。"

"您说的对，教授，"我说，"但我想知道更多的东西。"

在这一瞬间，我想实现一个夙愿，想弄明白人体是如何被创造出来的重大秘密。

沃尔德曼教授只看到我非常兴奋，但他并不知道我真正想做的事。他对我说，"维克多，你的想法让我很是欣慰。我坚信你会成为一位伟大的科学家。你在此学习期间如果需要任何帮助，我都会给予你的。"在以后的两年

understanding: *n.* 理解；懂得

23

give you all the help you need while you are here." During the next two years, Professor Waldman became my friend as well as my teacher. I read many books on science, and went to many talks on the subject. I met with all the great scientists at my school. Soon, I created a workroom in my house and worked there every night until dawn. One day, Professor Waldman called me into his workroom. "Victor, your progress has been amazing these past two years," he said proudly.

"Thank you, sir. I spend many hours studying the subjects of *anatomy* and *physiology*, so that one day I will know how human life begins. But I must first learn how life ends — how the body dies." "This will be very difficult, for you, Victor. Scientists have been trying to learn these things for many hundreds of years. You are a good scientist, and I believe that one day you will be truly great. If anyone can learn these things, you can. But do not forget the people who love you. Do you realize that you have not gone home in two years?" "Well, Professor, my work is too important to me right

24

中，沃尔德曼教授既是我的良师，也是我的挚友。我读了大量的科学书籍，并参加了许多有关科学主题的讲座。我拜访过大学里所有伟大的科学家。不久，我在住处建立了一间工作室，并在里面夜以继日地工作。一天，沃尔德曼教授把我叫到他的工作室。他自豪地说："维克多，这两年里你的进步太惊人了。"

"谢谢您，先生。我用了大量的时间研究解剖学和生理学，为的是有一天我能清楚人的生命是如何开始的。但我必须首先明白生命如何结束——人体怎样死亡。" "维克多，这对你是极为艰难的。几千年来科学家们一直试图搞明白这些事情。你是一位优秀的科学家，而且我坚信总有一天你一定会成为一位伟人。如果这个世界有一个人能弄明白这些事，那这个人就是你。但不要忘记那些爱你的人。你知道你都有两年没回过家了吗？" "啊，教授，我的研究目前实在太重要了，我没有时间回家。"我说。教授看起来很严肃，但没再说什么。在以后的几个月里，我在教堂的停尸房里度过了许多个夜晚，直到那些尸体下葬为止。我必须弄清楚一个人死后，死神是怎样用几天、几周和几年去改变尸体的。为了做到这一点，我在

25

ə'nætəmi

anatomy: n. 解剖学

physiology: n. 生理学

fizi'ɔlədʒi

now. I don't have time to go home," I said. The professor looked serious, but did not say anything more. The next few months, I spent many nights in the church buildings where the dead bodies were kept, until they were put into the ground. I needed to know how death changed the human body, in the days, weeks, and years after a person died. To learn these things, I visited *graveyards* on dark nights. I dug up dead bodies and studied them. Finally, after many months of study, an amazing idea came to me. In one moment, I suddenly understood not only how life turned into death... but also how death could be beaten, and turned back into life!

My thoughts and ideas excited me, but also frightened me, because they were so strange and new. I asked myself, "Why didn't great scientists of the old days learn these things? Instead, it is I, Victor, who has found the secret of all death and life!"

From that moment on, I began to work even harder. I slept and ate little. I had learned how life began, but now I was able to create life, from

漆黑的夜晚潜入墓地，掘出死尸，仔细观察。最后，经过数月的潜心研究，一个惊人的念头进入了我的脑海。在这一瞬间，我不但突然明白了生命怎样走向死亡……也明白了怎样击败死神，变死为生。

我的想法和念头使我兴奋，但也使我恐惧，因为它们太怪异、太新奇了。我问自己，"为什么以前的科学家们没有弄清楚这些事情，而偏偏是我——维克多发现了这个生与死的秘密？"

从此，我更加努力地工作。我几乎不吃不睡，我已经掌握了生命开始的秘密。但现在我能从已死亡的生物中再次创造出生命。这个狂

graveyard: n. 墓地（通常在教堂附近的一块地中）grave: n. 坟墓 [习语] from the cradle to grave 从生到死 turn in one's grave 死后不得安生

things that were already dead! The joy I felt made me forget how hard my life had been, and how much I missed my family. I could only think about my great discovery, which would make me famous.

At this point in Frankenstein's story, Robert Walton interrupted. "Amazing!" he said. "What is this great secret to creating life? Are you about to tell me?" Frankenstein shook his head. "I will not do that, Walton. Listen to the rest of my story. You have saved my life, and because of this, I can never *share* that knowledge with you. If you knew what I know, you would want to use the knowledge. Then you would destroy yourself, just like I have."

Walton said nothing more.

喜令我忘记了我过的日子是如何的艰苦，也忘了我有多么想家了。我惟一能想到的就是我那伟大的发现，它会使我成为名人。

　　弗兰肯斯坦讲到这里，罗伯特·沃尔顿打断了他的话。"太惊奇了！"他说，"创造生命的伟大秘密是什么？你打算告诉我吗？"弗兰肯斯坦摇了摇头。"沃尔顿，我不会告诉你，请听我下面的故事。你救了我的命，而正因如此，我才决不能让你分享我的知识。你要是掌握了我的知识，你一定会去使用这种知识。那么你就会像我一样，把自己毁灭掉。"

沃尔顿没再说话。

share: *v.* 分享 share sth. with sb. 与某人分享某物 *n.* 股份 buy 300 shares in a shipping company 买那个航运公司的 300股份

29

CHAPTER FOUR
The Monster

Why do I tell you that I am destroyed, like a dead man? I say it because the power that my knowledge gave me was too much for me, or any man. Men are weak — we are not strong like the gods. I asked myself some questions. I knew how to create life, but what kind of monster should I make? Did I want to create a simple animal monster, or a person like myself?

Soon, my head was full of wild dreams and ideas. I believed that nothing could stop me, and that I could do anything I wanted! Yes, I would build a monster that would be intelligent and wonderful, just like a human being! This monster would know that I had made it, and we would travel the world together. I knew that the monster could not be a normal size. This was because the human body is made up of so many parts. The monster would be *extremely* big, about eight feet tall. This

第四章
怪物

　　我为什么对你说我被毁灭了，已是行尸走肉了？我这样说，是因为我的知识给予我的力量，不论是在我还是他人看来，都太多了。人是弱者——我们不像神那样强大。我曾经问过自己一些问题。我知道自己能创造生命，但我该造出一个什么样的怪物呢？我是想造出一个简单的动物怪物，还是一个像我一样的人类怪物呢？

　　很快，我的脑海里便充满了各种疯狂的梦想和念头。我确信任何事情也阻止不了我，我能做到我想做的任何事情！是的，我要造出一个像人类一样聪明而且一样了不起的怪物！那个怪物要明白是我创造了他，我们可以一起去周游世界。我明白那个怪物不可能有人类的正常身材，因为构成人体的部件太多了。那个怪物会格外的高，高约八英尺。只有如此，我才能把所有的部件拼接起来。

extremely: adv. 极端地；极其地

way, I could put all the body parts together.

In the next months, I found all the things I would need. I took bones from dead bodies, and found animal parts. Then I found whole bodies that I dug up, from the graveyard near the church! It was summer when I began my work on the monster. Night after night, for more than a year, I would not stop my work. I forgot to eat, and slept little. I did not think about my family at all, even though Elizabeth and my father wrote me many letters. I only thought about myself — and the monster. Of course, sometimes I hated what I was doing. But most of the time I truly wanted to finish making the monster. It was winter when I knew my work was almost done. But by this time, I was extremely sick and tired. My body burned with fever. I was terribly thin, nothing but skin and bones. I never spoke to anyone and was always alone. But I did not *care about* my health. I said to myself, "Once I have made this monster, I will become healthy again, and see my family, and all the other good things!" How wrong I was.

在以后的几个月里，我找到了我所需要的所有部件。我从死尸上取下骨头，从动物身上取下各种部件。然后，我又从教堂附近的坟场中找出数个完整的尸体。我是在夏天开始造那个怪物的。日复一日，我不停地工作，一直忙了一年多。我几乎到了废寝忘食的地步。我一点也不想我的家人，尽管我的伊丽莎白和父亲给我写了很多信。我心中只有自己——还有那个怪物。当然，有时候我痛恨自己所做的事情。但大多数时间里，我真想完成创造那个怪物的工作。当我知道工作快完成时，已经到了冬季。这时我患了重病而且疲惫不堪。我发着高烧，极度消瘦，简直就是皮包骨头。我从不和任何人说话，总是独来独往。我毫不关心自己的身体，而是对自己说："一旦我大功告成，我就会康复的。我会去看自己的亲人和其他所有的美好事物。"我当时真是大错特错啊！

care about 关心。如：She didn't care about her husband. 她不关心她的丈夫。

33

CHAPTER FIVE
One Incredible Night

On a dark and *stormy* night in November the work was finally done. There was so much lightning that the room was as light as day. There was terrible thunder. Wind screamed and *howled* outside. The wild weather made me excited. I stared down at the table in my workroom, and thought about what I was about to do. On the table was an enormous monster, waiting to be given life. I touched the monster with my special tools. Because of the lightning, there was much electricity in the air. This electricity brought the monster to life! As I used my tools, the thunder and lightning were terrible. I screamed, "I command you to live! Live! Live!"

Slowly, the monster's eyes opened. They were ugly and yellow, like a snake's eyes. His large, strong arms and legs moved in the air.

I stared at this monster. I had spent two years

第五章
一个难以置信的夜晚

　　十一月一个漆黑的暴风雨之夜，所有的工作终于都完成了。空中的闪电一道接着一道，把屋子照得亮如白昼。雷声震耳，狂风怒号。但这恶劣的天气却令我兴奋不已。我俯视着工作间的桌子，思考着接下来要做什么。桌上躺着一个巨大的怪物，正等着我赐予生命。我把特制的仪器接在了怪物身上。由于闪电不断，空气大量带电，而这些电能会使这怪物活起来。我使用那些仪器时，雷电极为可怖。我喝道："我命令你活过来！活过来！活过来！"

　　怪物缓缓地睁开了双眼。这双眼呈黄色像蛇的眼睛一般，丑陋之极。他那粗大强壮的四肢也开始活动起来。

　　我凝视着这个怪物，它是我耗了两年心血

stormy: adj. 暴风雨的；热切的；激烈的 stormy weather 有暴风雨的天气 stormy discussion 激烈的讨论

howl: v. （动物的）嚎叫

of my life making him. Once, I had thought he was beautiful, because he had come from my life's dreams. But now, I only felt horror and fear. He was an ugly monster, made from death!

I saw huge, strong bones and muscles under his yellow skin. He had long, black hair, and an ugly face. His sharp, white teeth and thick black mouth were the most terrible! What had I done? I could not *stand* to look at the thing for another minute. I ran out of the workroom, and down to my bedroom. I hoped the monster would not follow me. I fell onto the bed, with all my clothes on. All I wanted to do was sleep. I hoped that when I woke up, I would find that everything had been a bad dream. When I finally fell asleep, I had terrible dreams about the monster, Elizabeth, and my mother. Suddenly I woke up. I had the feeling that something was watching me! The light of the moon came through the bedroom window. As my eyes opened, I saw the monster standing next to my bed. His black mouth moved and he gave me a terrible, ugly smile. He said some things that I did not un-

36

创造出来的。因为他出自我一生的梦想，我一度觉得他很美。但现在，我感到的只有恐怖和畏惧，因为他是由死尸制造的一个丑陋的怪物。

我看到的是黄色皮肤下的巨大而强壮的骨骼和肌肉、一头黑色长发及丑陋之极的脸，最可怕的是那肥厚的黑色大口和满口尖利的白牙。我都做了些什么啊？我无法再忍受看那怪物一眼。我冲出了工作室，跑进楼下的卧室，希望那个怪物不要跟着我。我和衣倒在床上，我需要的一切就是睡上一觉。我希望在醒来时，所有这一切都只不过是场噩梦。我入睡后，却做起了噩梦，梦到了那个怪物、伊丽莎白和我的母亲。我突然惊醒，感觉有什么东西正在注视着我。月光透过了卧室的窗户，我睁开眼睛时，发现站在我床前的竟是那个怪物。他动了动大黑嘴巴，狰狞地一笑。他用一种死人般的声音说了一些我根本听不懂的话，然后伸手来触摸我。我大叫一声从床上跳起并冲出了住所。那一夜，我躲在外面的一棵树下，虚弱不堪、惊魂未定、极其心烦意乱。我就这样熬过了那个的漆黑夜晚。

stand: *v.* 支持；忍耐；经住考验

derstand in a voice like death. Then his hand moved to touch me! Screaming, I jumped out of my bed and ran out of the apartment. That night, I hid outside under a tree, weak, frightened, and terribly upset, for the rest of that dark night.

CHAPTER SIX
Madness!

At six o'clock the next morning, my clothes wet with the rain, I walked slowly through the streets of the town. I did not know where to go or what to do. I was too afraid to go back to my house, and I thought that any minute I would see the monster on the streets, running towards me. I was standing on a street, watching *a coach and horses* come into the city. The door of the coach opened, and someone got out. When I saw him, I cried out in surprise. It was my best friend, Henry Clerval.

"Victor!" he cried. "How wonderful to see you here!" Even though I was still thinking about the monster, I was so happy to see Henry that I began to feel a little better. "Somehow, I will make things better," I said to myself as we walked down the street towards my house. Henry told me why he had come. "My father finally agreed that I should

第六章
疯狂

第二天早上六点钟，我穿着被雨打湿的衣服，缓缓地穿过城市的街道。我既不知要到哪儿去也不知要做什么。我吓得不敢返回住所，而且觉得随时都会在街上看到那个怪物向我冲过来。我站在街上，看到一辆由几匹马拉的马车进了城。马车的门打开了，一个人走了下来。我一见到他，不禁惊叫一声，那正是我最好的朋友——亨利·克勒瓦尔。

"维克多！"他喊道。"在这儿见到你真是太好了！"尽管我仍在想着那个怪物，但见到亨利后我十分高兴，马上感觉好些了。我们一起走向我的住所时，我对自己说，"无论如何，我一定会把事情处理好的。"亨利对我说了他来这儿的原因，"我父亲终于同意让我去学习并看看这个世界，不再每天为他工作，所以我现在来上大学了。"我对他说，"亨利，这实在是太棒了，有你在此相伴真是太好了。

a coach and horses: 一辆由几匹马拉的马车

41

study and see the world, instead of just working for him all the time. So now I can go to the university." "Henry, this is wonderful," I told him. "It will be good to have you here with me. Do you have any news of my family? How are they?

"Your father, Elizabeth, and your brothers are all well, but they have not *heard from* you in a long time. They are worried, Victor. You should write them!" He stopped walking and looked at me. "Now that I see you, I am worried too. You are too thin and pale — you look sick!" "Don't worry, I'm not sick," I said. "I have been working on something, but it's over now. I can finally rest." When I saw my apartment, I felt terribly afraid again. What if the monster was still in my bedroom? What if it tried to hurt Henry and me? What would Henry think if he saw the monster?

I ran up the stairs ahead of my friend. As I opened the door to my apartment, my heart stopped. But, thank God, the monster was not there. I let Henry come inside.

My happiness that the monster was gone was so

你有我家里的消息吗？他们都好吗？"

"你的父亲、伊丽莎白和你的弟弟们都很好，但他们好久没有收到你的信了，很担心你。维克多，你应该给他们写封信！"他停下脚步，看着我，"既然我看到你，也为你担心。因为你太瘦了，脸色太苍白了，你看来是病了。""别担心，我没病，"我说，"我一直在忙着做一件事，但现在已经做完了，我终于可以休息了。"当我看到我的住所时，我又害怕起来。要是那个怪物还在我卧室里怎么办？他要是想伤害亨利和我那怎么办？亨利若见到那个怪物会怎么想呢？

我抢在亨利前面跑上台阶。当我打开住处的门时，我的心都停止了跳动。但是，真要感谢上帝，那个怪物不在里面。我让亨利进了屋。

怪物不在屋内真是让我太高兴了，我开始

hear from: 收到某人的来信

great, that I began to laugh loudly, jumping over chairs and shaking my hands like a wild man. Henry was frightened.

Henry grabbed me and began to shake me. "Victor, stop it! What is wrong? You really are sick! What is it?"

My body began to shake. My tired brain thought it saw the monster walking into the room. "He is the cause!" I shouted, pointing to the door. Of course, nothing was really there. "Henry, save me!" Henry tried to throw me onto the bed, but I thought it was the monster trying to hurt me. I fought Henry, hitting him until I fell down on the floor, screaming. I do not remember anything more after that. How frightened Henry was to see me acting this way. But I did not know this, because for many months I was terribly sick. Henry never told my family, because he knew my father and Elizabeth would worry. My friend took care of me himself for many days, and no one has ever done anything more kind and brave. During my sickness, I talked in my sleep many times. I would talk about

放声大笑，从椅子上跳过来跳过去，并像野人一样挥动着双臂。亨利吓坏了。

他抓住我并摇晃我，"停下来，维克多！发生什么事了？你真的是病了，到底怎么了？"

我的身体开始颤抖。我疲倦的大脑，似乎看到怪物走了进来。于是我指着门喊道，"他就是造成这一切的罪魁祸首。亨利，快救我。"门口当然什么也没有，于是亨利试图扶我上床，但我却认为这是那个怪物要伤害我。于是我就和亨利打了起来，不停地打他，后来，我自己摔倒在地上，不停地尖叫着。别的事我就都记不起来了。看到我的样子，亨利真是吓坏了。但我并不知道这些，因为我一病数月。亨利没有告诉我的亲人，因为他知道我的父亲和伊丽莎白会担心的。我的朋友亲自照顾了我许多天，没有任何行为比他的行动更善良更勇敢了。在我患病期间，我不断地说梦话。我总是谈到那个怪物，我有多么地痛恨和害怕他。我说这些时亨利并不在意，他认为那是病人的胡话。五个多月后，我的身体真正地好转了。大病痊愈，心情也好多了。我慢慢地又恢复到了亨利所熟知的那个原来的我了。当然，他还是不知道我的所作所为。我知道我的生命和健康全是他给的，我简直不敢相信他是如此一位佳友。"亲爱的亨利，我怎么来感谢你呢？你本

the monster, and how much I hated and feared it. Henry did not *pay attention* when I said these things; he thought it was only my sick mind that caused me to talk in this way. After more than five months, I truly felt better. My body was healed, and my mind was better. Slowly, I was becoming the same person Henry had always known. Of course, he still did not know what I had done. I knew that I owed him my life and health, and I could not believe what a wonderful friend he was. "Dear Henry, how can I ever thank you? You have spent so many months taking care of me, when you might have been going to school. Your dream has been to study for many years now. How can I repay you?" "Victor, just take care of your health, and get well. And will you please go and see your family!" One day, I took Henry to my school, where he met my professors and some of the other students. When we met my favorite teacher, Professor Waldman, he told Henry, "Victor is the best student at this university. What a wonderful scientist he is! We *are* very *proud of* him!" The professor *meant* to

应该去上大学，却一直照顾了我好几个月。你多年的梦想就是学习，我该怎样回报你呢？""维克多，关心自己的身体，赶快康复，并请你一定去看看家里的亲人。"一天，我带亨利到我的学校去，他在那儿见到了我的教授们和其他一些学生。当我们见到我最喜爱的老师——沃尔德曼教授时，他告诉亨利，"维克多是这所大学里最棒的学生，他是一个极好的科学家，我们为他感到自豪。"教授是想在我大病初愈后让我高兴，但我却痛苦不堪。因为我，这个全校"最棒的"学生创造出了一个可怕的怪物。当教授谈到我时，亨利看到了我的脸色。他并没问我是怎么回事，相反他开始谈论其他的事情，我才觉得好了一些。我爱亨利就像爱自己的弟弟一样，我也迫切地想询问一个人到底应该怎么办。但我知道我决不能告诉他我的所作所为。如果我这样做的话，他就会和我一样地痛苦与恐惧。

pay attention (to sb./sth.): 注意到某人/某物

be proud of sb./sth.: 为某人/某物而骄傲 be proud to do sth. 为做某事而骄傲 [谚语] as proud as a peacock 趾高气扬

mean: v. 意思是；意味着 mean sb. to do sth. 意欲让某人干某事 mean well 处于善意

47

make me happy after my long sickness, but I felt miserable. Because I, the university's "best student," had created a terrible monster! Henry saw the look on my face when the Professor talked about me. He did not ask me what was wrong, but instead began to talk of other things. I felt a little better. I loved Henry like a brother, and I deeply wanted to ask someone what to do. But I knew I could never tell him what I had done. If I did so, he would feel the pain and fear that I felt.

Soon, I decided to stop my study of science. It had *brought* too much struggle and horror into my life. I could not even go into my workroom and use my tools. Henry saw my pain, but, like a good friend, he never asked me questions. However, I decided to stay in school and study Oriental languages with Henry, because I did not want to go home and do nothing. Together, we spent a happy year studying new languages. We read the beautiful, strange books of Persian writers. We took long walks in the forests around the town of Ingolstadt. Often, we would leave school for many days, sleeping in strange houses and towns. With time, I became a happy person again. I was able to forget the monster and my sickness, as if it had all been a bad dream.

不久，我决定停止科学研究。它给我的生活带来了太多的艰辛和恐惧。我甚至无法到工作室去使用那些仪器。亨利看出了我的痛苦，但他就像一个真正的好友那样，从来不向我发问。然而，我却打算留在学校里和亨利一起研究东方语言，因为我既不想回家，也不想无所事事。我们一起学习新的语言，一起度过了愉快的一年。我们一起阅读波斯作家那些优美而又奇异的书籍；我们一起到英格尔斯塔特城周围的森林中去远足；我们经常离开学校许多天，在奇特的房舍和城镇中过夜。随着时间的推移，我又成了一个愉快的人，我已能够忘掉那个怪物和我的疾病，就像那是一场噩梦一样。

bring: *v.* 带来 bring about 导致。如：The war brings about the reform. 战争导致了改革。

ing in strange houses and towns. With time, I became a happy person again. I was able to forget the monster, and my sickness, as if it had all been a bad dream.

CHAPTER SEVEN
A Murder Occurs

I t was a beautiful morning in May. Henry and I had just come back from a long walk in the country. On the table in our house, there was a letter from my father. I wondered what he was writing about, because I was going to visit my family soon, after many years away. "Can't he wait until he sees me, to talk to me about it?" I thought.

Quickly, I opened the letter and read these words.

Geneva, May 12

My son,

It is with great sadness and pain that I tell you: you must come home now. But first, I must tell you what has happened here. Sit down in a chair before you read my next words. Your little brother, William, is dead. My happy young boy has been murdered. Victor, I will not try to comfort you. I will only tell you what happened.

第七章
一场凶杀案发生了

这是五月的一个美好的上午，我和亨利刚从乡间远足回来。在我们住处的桌子上有一封父亲寄来的信。我想知道信里写了些什么，因为离家多年后我正打算不久以后就回家看看。"难道他就等不到我回家时再说吗？"我想。

我很快打开信，看到了以下内容。

日内瓦 五月十二日

我的儿：

我极度悲伤而痛苦地告诉你，你现在必须回来，但首先我要告诉你发生了什么事。读下面内容前先找张椅子坐下。你的弟弟——威廉死了。我那快乐的小儿子被人杀害了。维克多，我不想试图去安慰你，我只想告诉你到底发生了什么事。

Last Thursday in the evening, your two brothers, Elizabeth, and I went for a walk in the forest of Plainpalais. You loved to run and play here when you were a child. On that evening, William and Ernest were far away from Elizabeth and I, playing games. It began to get dark, and Elizabeth and I sat down to wait for the boys. Soon, Ernest came to us and asked if we had seen William. Ernest told us that William had gone to hide, but he had not returned. Immediately, Elizabeth and I began to look for William. But we had not found him after three hours of searching. Elizabeth ran home to tell the servants to look for William around the house. At five o'clock in the morning, I finally found him. His cold, dead body was lying on the grass, and there were black finger marks on his throat! I carried him home and put him on his bed. When Elizabeth ran into the room and saw him, she screamed out, "Oh, my God! I have killed my darling William..." and she fainted onto the floor. When we woke her up, she told me that yesterday, William had asked to wear Elizabeth's necklace. The necklace was a beautiful gold one. Elizabeth couldn't say no to William. But when she saw William's body, there was no necklace around

上星期四傍晚，我和你的两个弟弟及伊丽莎白一起到普兰帕莱森林中去散步。你还是个孩子时也喜欢到那儿去奔跑玩耍。那天傍晚威廉和厄内斯特离开伊丽莎白和我去做游戏。天渐渐黑了，我和伊丽莎白坐下等那两个孩子。不久，厄内斯特回来了，问我们是否见到威廉。他说威廉跑去藏起来，但还没有回来。我和伊丽莎白立刻开始找威廉，但我们找了三个小时也未找到。伊丽莎白跑回家去，叫仆人们到院子周围去找他。早上五点钟，我终于找到了他。他那冰冷的尸体躺在草地上，喉头上有几个黑色的手指印。我把他背回家，并把他放在他的床上。伊丽莎白跑进屋里，一看到他，就高叫起来，"噢，上帝啊！是我害死了亲爱的威廉……"接着就昏倒在地上。我们把她救醒后，她说威廉昨天要戴她的项链。那是条漂亮的金项链，而伊丽莎白无法拒绝。但当她看到威廉的尸体时，脖子上却没有了项链。伊丽莎白认为有人是为了那条项链而杀害了威廉。

play games 玩游戏 [辨] play the game 按部就班，一丝不苟 give the game away 露出马脚

his neck. *Elizabeth thought someone had killed William because they wanted the necklace.*

We have not found the murderer yet. Elizabeth blames herself for William's death, and cannot stop crying. We need you to come home, Victor. Not to find the killer, but to comfort our sad hearts.

Your loving father

Alphonse Frankenstein

I threw the letter across the room, covered my face with my hands, and began to cry.

Henry ran into the room and asked me, "My dear friend, what has happened?" I couldn't speak; I could only point to the letter lying on the floor. As Henry read the letter, he cried out in pain, and tears fell from his eyes.

我们还没有找到凶手。伊丽莎白为威廉的死而自责，她一直在哭泣。我们需要你回来。维克多，不是要你找出凶手，而是为了安慰我们那悲伤的心。

爱你的父亲

艾尔封斯·弗兰肯斯坦

我将信扔到屋子的另一头，双手掩面，哭了起来。

亨利跑进屋里问我，"我亲爱的朋友，发生了什么事？"我说不出话，只是指了指地上的那封信。亨利看着信，痛苦地哭了出来，泪水滚滚而下。

blame: *v.* 责备；训斥 blame sb. for sth./doing sth. 因某事训斥某人 [谚语] A bad workman blames his tools. 工拙怨械笨。

CHAPTER EIGHT
The Figure in the Woods

I left for Geneva that day. It was a sad, horrible journey. All I thought about was my sweet little brother, and the pain my family must be feeling. They had lost my mother, and now William, so soon! But as I came near to Geneva, I became afraid. When I arrived at the gates of the city it was very late. In my sadness, I had forgotten that people could not enter the gates after ten o'clock at night. I decided to find a room for the night at an inn on Lake Geneva. I could not sleep, so I found a boat and *sailed* across the lake. The Plainpalais forest, where William had died, was on the other side of the lake. For some reason, I wanted to see the place where my brother had been killed. "Maybe there will be a clue there," I thought. Close by, I could see a storm in the mountains. By the time I had reached the forest, rain had begun to fall. There was loud thunder, and so much lightning

第八章
林中的身影

当天我就启程赴日内瓦。这一路真是既难
受而又可怕。我脑中所想的全是我那快乐的弟
弟和亲人们正在遭受的痛苦。他们已经失去了
我的母亲，现在又这么快就失去了威廉。但当
我来到日内瓦附近时，我害怕起来。我到城门
口时，天已经很晚了。我沉浸于悲伤之中，竟
忘了晚上十点之后是不许进城的。于是我决定
到日内瓦湖上的一家客栈去找个房间过夜。但
我无法入睡，所以我找了一条小船划过湖去。
威廉被害的地点——普兰帕莱斯森林，就在湖
对岸。出于某种原因，我想到威廉被害的地点
去看一看。"那儿也许会有点线索。"我想。
我走到近前时发现山中正酝酿着一场暴风雨。
我刚步入森林，马上便下起雨来。雷声阵阵，
道道闪电将天空照得如同白昼一般。当我走出
小船上岸时，我看到附近有一个人影，当那个
人影从树后走出时，我静静地站在那儿，想看
看那是谁。

sail: *v.* 航行 sail through 顺利
通过。如：She sails through
the important exams.她顺利通
过了这次重要考试。

in the sky that it seemed like daytime. When I stepped out of my boat onto the ground, I saw the figure of a man near me. As the figure stepped out from behind a tree, I stood still, trying to see whom it was.

The next flash of lightning *lit up* the sky. Then I saw him. It wasn't a man — it was the monster I had created! After one year, what was he doing here? Then I had a horrible thought. Suddenly, I knew the answer to my question. The monster had killed my brother, an innocent little boy! I was so upset that I had to lean against a tree so that I would not fall down. When I looked up, I saw the monster running away. I tried to follow him, but he moved extremely fast. I saw him begin to climb a mountain. Then he was gone, into the darkness.

I stood against the tree, remembering the night I had given the monster life. I was filled with pain as I thought, "Did I create this thing so that it could kill? What other terrible thing has it done? Oh, my God!" I ran through the forest all night looking for the creature. When morning came, I

又一道闪电划破夜空，我看清了他。那不是一个人——那是我创造的那个怪物！一年过去了，他在这儿干什么？接着我心中冒出一个可怕的念头，我突然对我的问题得出了答案。怪物杀死了我的弟弟——一个天真无邪的男孩。我难过极了，不得不靠在一棵树上免得摔倒。等我抬起头来，那怪物已经跑远了。我想追上他，但他跑得太快了。我看到他开始爬上一座山，然后消失在黑暗之中。

我靠在树干上，想起了我赐予怪物生命的那个夜晚。我越想越痛苦，"我创造出这家伙是叫他来杀人的吗？他还干过些什么恶行呢？啊，我的上帝。"我整夜地在林中奔走，寻找那个家伙。天亮后，我到了父亲的家中。我想把这件事告诉警察。他们也许能找到那个怪物。但我怎么告诉他们呢？我真地能说，是

lit up: 容光奕奕

61

went to my father's house. I thought about telling the police my story. Perhaps they could find the monster. But what story would I tell them? Could I really say that I, a young student, had created a horrible monster from dead human bodies? Could I tell them I had seen that same monster in the woods last night? The police would never believe me. Besides, who would believe such a strange tale from a man who had spent many months sick and almost insane?

I knew that if someone tried to tell me this kind of story, I would not have believed it. I would think he was sick. And no one could stop or kill a monster that was as large and strong as this one. I had no answers, so I said nothing.

我——一个年轻的大学生，用死人的尸体创造出一个可怕的怪物吗？我能说我昨夜在林中见到了同一个怪物吗？警察是绝不会相信的。另外，谁又会相信一个一病数月、几乎精神失常的人讲的这样一个离奇的故事呢？

我清楚即便有人试图给我讲这种故事，我也不会相信的。我会认为他不正常。另外谁也无法制止或杀死像这样一个高大强壮的怪物。我找不到任何答案，所以我什么也没说。

CHAPTER NINE
Searching for a Killer

When I arrived at my father's house it was early in the morning. Quietly I told the servants not to wake my family, because they needed to rest. I went to the library and looked at the painting of my dear mother on the wall. A painting of William was next to it. I held my sweet brother's picture to my heart and began to cry. At that moment, my brother Ernest ran into the library. We threw our arms around each other and began to cry.

After a little while, I asked how Elizabeth and my father were feeling. I asked how my father and Elizabeth were bearing up.

"Father is hiding his sadness and anger from us. But Elizabeth has been miserable. She had blamed herself for William's death, but now we have found the real killer!" Before I had time to think, I cried out, "You have found the killer! That is impossible! I saw him last night on the

第九章
寻找凶手

我是一大早赶到父亲家的。我悄悄地告诉仆人们不要叫醒家里人，因为他们需要休息。我到书房里去看墙上挂着的我亲爱的母亲的画像。威廉的画像紧挨着它。我把我那可爱的弟弟的肖像抱在胸前开始哭起来。就在这时，我的弟弟厄内斯特冲进书房，我们拥抱在一起，抱头痛哭。

过了一会，我问弟弟父亲和伊丽莎白现在如何，他们如何承受痛苦的。

"父亲把悲伤和愤怒藏在心里。但伊丽莎白的情况可就不好了。她一直为威廉的死而自责。不过现在，我们已找到了真正的凶手。"我不假思索就脱口而出，"你们已经找到了凶手？这是不可能的！昨晚我在那座山上见过他，他仍然逍遥法外！"

bear up: 忍耐；坚持bear up against 忍耐

65

mountain, and he was still free!"

Luckily for me, my brother only said, "I don't know what you mean, Victor. We have found the killer, and it has only made us unhappier. It was our servant girl, Justine, who killed William." "Justine?" I gasped. "But..."

"I know what you are thinking. We didn't believe it, at first. Elizabeth still doesn't believe Justine is the killer. And truthfully, the facts are very strange. Another servant found Elizabeth's necklace in Justine's pocket. The servant did not talk to us first, but went to the police immediately. Then the police came and arrested Justine. Her *trial* is tomorrow." "Ernest, I know she's innocent!" I cried. "I promise you, I know who the real killer is!"

Ernest could not ask me any more questions because at that moment, my father and Elizabeth came into the room. My father told me the rest of the story. "We don't want to believe that Justine is the killer, because she has worked for our family for many years. She loved your mother and

幸运的是，我弟弟只是说出下面的话：
"维克多，我不懂你是什么意思。我们已经找
到了凶手，但这却令我们更加难过。杀害威廉
的是我们侍女，朱斯汀。""朱斯汀？"我简直
喘不过气来。"但是……"

"我知道你在想什么。一开始我们也不相
信，伊丽莎白到现在还是不信朱斯汀是凶手。
而且事实上，事情非常奇怪。一个仆人在朱斯
汀的口袋里发现了伊丽莎白的项链。那个仆人
没有先告诉我们，而是马上报告了警察。警察
随后就来逮捕朱斯汀了。明天要对她进行审
判。""厄内斯特，我知道她是无辜的。"我喊
道，"我向你发誓，我知道真正的凶手是谁!"

厄内斯特无法再向我发问，因为这时候我
父亲和伊丽莎白走进了房间。父亲给我继续讲
事情的原委。"我们不愿相信朱斯汀是凶手，
因为她已在我们家干了好多年啦。她爱你母亲
和威廉。我希望这件可怕的事不是真的，但我
们无能为力。我们得等着看法官怎么说。"伊
丽莎白一直等到父亲说完，才对我说，"亲爱

trial: *n.* 审判 stand trial for
sth. 因某事而接受审判

67

William. I hope that this terrible thing is not true. But we can do nothing. We must wait and see what the judges say." Elizabeth waited until my father had finished speaking, and then she said to me, "Darling, you must find a way to prove that Justine is not the killer! Justine could never kill anyone. And she has cared for William since he was a baby!"

的，你必须想法证明朱斯汀不是凶手。朱斯汀不会杀任何人的，威廉是朱斯汀看着长大的。"

CHAPTER TEN
The Second Victim

The next day I went to the courthouse with Elizabeth, Ernest and my father. More than anything, I wanted to scream out that I had killed my brother, so that Justine would not be punished. And, if you think about it, this was the truth. But I knew that everyone would think I was crazy. I had not even been in Geneva at the time of the murder. Ernest had told me that there was no real *proof* that Justine had killed William. That day, the police took Justine into the courtroom and she began to tell her story. She said that when Elizabeth told her William was lost, she ran to the forest to try and find him. After many hours, she tried to go home, but the city gates were closed. Justine had to sleep in a barn near the gates. She was so tired that she fell asleep in a few minutes. Justine promised all the people in the room that she did not know why the necklace, which had been on

第十章
第二个牺牲品

第二天，我、伊丽莎白、厄内斯特和父亲一道去了法庭。我最想做的事就是想高喊是我杀了自己的弟弟，以使朱斯汀免受惩罚。而且，如果你仔细想的话，实情确实如此。但我也知道这样一来人人都会认为我是个疯子。因为凶杀案发生时我并不在日内瓦。厄内斯特已对我说过没有真凭实据证明是朱斯汀杀害了威廉。那天，警察把朱斯汀带上法庭后，她开始

陈述。她说那天当伊丽莎白说威廉失踪后，她就跑进森林里并试图找到他。数小时后她想回家，但城门已经关闭。她只得在城门口的一个谷仓里过夜。她太累了，几分钟后就沉沉睡去。朱斯汀向法庭上所有的人发誓她不知道为什么威廉脖子上的项链会在她的衣袋中。她多次说这肯定是真正的凶手放进去的。"但这会是谁呢？"她问所有在场的人，"我没有仇人。如果凶手是为了那条项链而杀害了威廉，为什么他又把它放进我的口袋里呢？"伊丽莎白站起来告诉法官们朱斯汀是一个非常善良的好姑娘，她请法官释放她。但我却看到了法官们脸上的怒气，因为他们已认定她就是凶手。突然我听到朱斯汀承认她是凶手。我不明白她为什么这样说。我冲出了法庭，我没法再去听更多的话了。是我创造的怪物做下了这桩事，在

proof: *n.* 证据

William's neck, was in the pocket of her dress. She told us many times that the real killer must have put it there. "But who is he?" she asked the people in the room. "I do not have any enemies. And if a person killed William just to have the necklace, why did the killer then leave it in my pocket?" Elizabeth stood up and told the judges that Justine was a good, wonderful girl. She asked the judges to let her go. But I saw the angry look on the judges' faces. They already thought she was the killer. Then I heard Justine suddenly *confess* that she was the killer. I did not know why she said so. I ran out of the courtroom. I could not listen to any more talk. I had made the monster that had done this thing. In a way, I was the killer.

A short while later, Elizabeth and my father came out. Their faces were white, and my father looked a hundred years older.

"Oh, Victor," cried Elizabeth, "I can't believe what is happening." She threw herself into my arms. I hated myself so much at that moment that I did not want to touch her.

某种意义上，我才是凶手。

又过了一会儿，伊丽莎白和父亲也走了出来。他们脸色苍白，而父亲好像百岁老人。

"噢，维克多，"伊丽莎白哭道，"我无法相信这件事。"她投入到我的怀抱，而我当时正深深怨恨着自己，根本不想碰她一下。

confess: *v.*忏悔 confess (to) sth./(to) doing sth. 忏悔干过某事 confess sth. to sb. 向某人忏悔干过某事

"First Justine told us she was innocent. Now she tells us that she killed William!" my father shouted. "No!" I cried. "I won't believe this!"

Just then, a man came out and to Elizabeth, "Miss Lavenza, the killer asks to talk to you."

Elizabeth turned to me. "Victor, I must talk to her, even if she is the killer. I can't go in alone. Please come with me." I did not want to see Justine, but I could not say no. Justine was sitting in a locked room. Her hands were tied, and she was praying.

When she saw us, she cried bitterly. "Justine, how could you lie to us? I never thought you could kill anyone. But you told them you had done it." "Oh, Miss Elizabeth, I did tell them I was the killer," cried Justine. "But it is all a lie! They told me I had to confess, because they were going to blame me anyway. They said if I didn't confess the crime, I wouldn't go to heaven. But I didn't do it. I could not die with you thinking I had killed our dear, sweet child!" Justine stared out of the window. "I've told you the truth, and now I

"开始，朱斯汀对我们说她是无辜的，但现在她却说是她杀害了威廉。"父亲高声说。"不！"我喊道，"我绝不相信。"

就在这时，一个人从法庭里走出来找伊丽莎白，"拉凡萨小姐，凶手要求和您讲话。"

伊丽莎白转过头来对我说："维克多，即使她真是凶手，我也要跟她谈谈。我无法单独去，请你陪我一起去。"我不想见朱斯汀，但我无法说不。朱斯汀坐在一间上了锁的屋里；她的手被捆着；她正在祈祷。

她一见到我们，就痛哭起来。"朱斯汀，你怎么能对我们说谎呢？我认为你不会杀任何人，但你却对他们说你杀了人。""噢，伊丽莎白小姐，我确实对他们说我是凶手，"朱斯汀哭道。"但那全是谎言！他们对我说我必须认罪，因为无论如何他们都要归罪于我。他们说如果我不承认这桩罪行，我就进不了天堂。但我没杀人，我绝不能死了还让你们认为是我杀了那个可亲可爱的孩子。"朱斯汀凝视着窗外，"我已经对你们讲了实情，现在我可以平静地死去了。你们明白……而且上帝也明白……我是无辜的！"伊丽莎白冲过去抱住了朱斯汀。两个女人哭成一团。我却无法用语言来安慰她们。我和伊丽莎白去找法官谈了好几个

can die peacefully. You know... and God knows... I am innocent! " Elizabeth ran and put her arms around Justine, and both women began to cry. I could say nothing to comfort them. Elizabeth and I spent many hours talking to the judges, but it did no good. Early the next morning, Justine was hung as a killer. Now two people had died because of my terrible monster: William and Justine. " I don't want to live anymore," I told myself. " Killing myself may be the answer, but I cannot hurt Elizabeth, Ernest, and my father even more." Most importantly of all, I did not know if the monster would try to hurt my family again. I needed to watch and protect them. I promised myself, "One day, I shall find this monster and look him in the face. Then I shall make him *pay for* his terrible crimes!"

小时，但无济于事。第二天一早，朱斯汀就作为凶手被绞死了。现在已有两个人——威廉和朱斯汀——都死于我创造的那个怪物之手。"我不想再活下去了，"我自言自语地说："杀死我自己可能是个解决问题的方法。但我不能再伤害伊丽莎白、厄内斯特和我的父亲。"更重要的是，我不知道那个怪物是否会再次伤害我的亲人。我需要看护他们，保护他们。我默默地发誓："有一天，我要找到这个怪物，当面讨个说法，然后我要让他为自己的恶行付出代价。"

pay for: 付出代价 [搭配] pay the price for sth. 为某事而付出代价

CHAPTER ELEVEN
Face to Face with the Monster

After Justine's death, it was hard for me to spend time with my family, because I felt that everything that had happened was my *fault*. I decided to travel alone to a peaceful town in the mountains. I took long walks in the beautiful fields and looked at the mountains in the moonlight. After a month of this, I was able to sleep well at night. One rainy day I went to my favorite spot on the mountain. I did this every day, in good weather and bad. I liked to watch the glaciers, which were large pieces of ice, break and fall down the mountain.

As my horse slowly walked up the path the rain continued to fall. Finally I arrived at the top of the mountain. But today, instead of resting I decided to cross the great ice. The glacier was covered with holes and cracks, so it was dangerous. It took me two hours to reach the other side. Finally the rain stopped and the sun came out. The ice

第十一章
直面怪物

朱斯汀死后，我很难和家里人一起生活，因为我觉得这一切都是我的错。我决定单独旅行，到群山中一个安宁的小镇去。我在美丽的田野中远足，观看月光下的山景。一个月后，晚上我能睡安稳了。一个雨天，我去了山上我最喜欢的地方。无论天气好坏，我每天都到那儿去。我喜欢观看冰川，看巨大的冰块碎裂并坠入山谷。

我骑马缓缓地沿山路上山时，雨还在下着。我终于到了山顶。但这一天，我不想休息，而是想从冰川上走过去。冰川上到处是洞和裂缝，走在上面很危险。我用了两个小时才走到另一边。最终雨过天晴，冰川闪烁着五颜六色的光芒。我看着眼前的美景，感觉愉快多了。突然，我看到一个异常高大的人快步向我走来。他从冰川上跑过，就像在草地上飞跑一样。我由于愤怒和恐惧而浑身发抖：这正是那

fault: *n*. 错误。例如：He seldom makes any fault in his work.他的工作很少出错。

79

sparkled and shone in the light. I watched the beautiful sight and felt a little happier. Suddenly I saw an extremely large man walking quickly towards me. He ran over the ice as if it was only grass. I shook with anger and *fright*. It was the monster. Finally, we would meet after two years. At that moment, I knew that I would not turn and run away from him. I had to stay and fight him until one of us died, if I could. It was the only way to end the fear and pain in my life!

"You monster!" I shouted. " Go to hell! I wish I could kill you, and bring back the two people you killed from heaven!" "I am not surprised that you say these things, Dr. Frankenstein. I thought you would," the monster said calmly. "After all, people hate ugly things, and I am ugly. But this is your fault, because you created me this way."

Where had the monster learned to speak so well? I could not believe what I was hearing. But I did not stop to think, because I could not control my anger any more. I ran and tried to hit his awful,

个怪物。两年了，我们终于又见面了。当时我明白我绝不能转身从他面前跑掉。如果我能的话，我要和他搏斗，直到其中一个死掉为止。只有这样才能消除我生活中的恐惧和痛苦。

"你这个怪物！"我高喊。"下地狱去吧！我希望我能把你杀掉，并从天堂里换回被你害死的那两个人。""你这样说我一点也不惊奇，弗兰肯斯坦博士，我早就认为你会这样说。"怪物平静地说。"无论如何，人们都讨厌丑陋的东西，而我就很丑陋。但这是你的过错，因为是你把我造成这个样子的。"

这怪物从哪儿学的这么会说话呢？我不敢相信我所听到的。但我没有停下来去想，因为我再也无法控制自己的愤怒。我冲过去，试图用双手去打他那张可恶的黄脸。

fright: *n.* 恐惧，恐怖
be filled with fright 充满恐惧

yellow face with my hands.

But the monster was too quick and strong. He grabbed my arm and said, "*Calm* yourself, creator. I expect you to listen to my story before you try to attack me again. Remember, you made me larger and stronger than you." "I won't listen! I don't want to hear anything you have to say!" The monster looked into my eyes. I shook with fear, a feeling I did not understand. "How can I make you understand, Victor Frankenstein? It is true that you have suffered. But this is nothing, when you understand how I have suffered. I am miserable and alone, hated by all people. This is all because of you." "Monster, say no more! I hate myself for having made you!"

"Then you must listen to what I have to say! Then, if you still want to kill me, you can try — if you can! Just remember, it was you who made me." "Please, I beg you, go away! I can't look at you a minute longer!" I cried. I turned my back to him and put my hands over my face.

"Then don't look at me. Please, Dr. Franken-

但怪物反应太快也太强壮了。他抓住我的胳膊说道，"平静些，创造我的人。我希望在你听完我的故事之前不要再来攻击我。请记住，是你把我造得比你又高又壮的。" "我不听！我不想听你说任何话！"怪物直盯着我的眼睛，我由于恐惧和一种难以言表的感觉而发抖。"我怎样才能使你明白呢，维克多·弗兰肯斯坦？不错，你是受了许多苦。但如果你明白我经受过怎样的痛苦时，你受的苦就微不足道了。我处境悲惨、孤苦伶仃、遭人痛恨。这全都是因为你。" "怪物，不要说了，我恨自己创造了你。"

"那你更得要听听我要说的话！然后，如果你还想杀死我，你可以试一试——如果你能的话！请记住，是你创造了我！" "请吧，我求你离开这儿。我一刻也不想再看到你！"我吼道。我转过身去，以手掩面。

"那么，就请你别看我，弗兰肯斯坦博士。

calm: *n.* 平静；镇定 [谚语] the calm before the storm 暴风雨到来前的平静 *adj.* 平静的 a calm sea 平静的大海

83

stein. Just listen to my story, and hear what I have to ask you. If you do what I ask, I promise you I will leave you in peace." Even though I was afraid, when I listened to the monster's deep voice I felt that I wanted to know more about him. I turned around and said, "I will listen." "Then come with me. I know of a shelter on that mountain where we can talk."

He turned and walked quickly across the ice. I followed slowly behind him. When I arrived at the shelter, the monster was inside making a fire. I sat down next to the fire and listened as the monster began to talk.

只听我讲我的故事，再听听我想求你做的事。如果你能答应我的请求，我保证再也不打扰你。"尽管我很害怕，但听了怪物那低沉的声音后，我觉得我想更多地了解他。我转过身来说道，"我愿意听。""那么，请跟我来，我知道山上有个小木屋，我们可以在那儿说话。"

他转身迅速地走过了冰川，我缓缓地跟在他身后。等我到达小木屋时，怪物已在里面生起了一堆火。我坐在火旁，听怪物开始讲述他的经历。

remember: v. 记着；记住[辨] remember doing sth.记住干过某事 remember to do sth. 记住要干某事

CHAPTER TWELVE
The Monster Speaks

W hen you first gave me life, I was like a small baby. I could not speak, but I could smell, hear, taste, feel, and see. I was frightened by everything I saw around me. I tried to go to you for help, like a child goes to his father. I could not speak to you, so you did not know what I wanted. You ran away and left me, and I did not know why.

I was cold, so I put on one of your coats and went out into the dark night. I *remember* crying as I walked through the streets. When I reached the forest I was very tired so I lay down on the ground near a little stream.

I slept for a few hours and when I woke up, I was hungry and thirsty. I drank some water from the stream and ate some small fruits I found on the ground. For a month I lived in that forest. I watched the sun and moon in the sky. I listened to

第十二章
怪物所讲的故事

您刚赐予我生命时，我就像一个初生的婴儿。我不会说话，但我有嗅觉、听觉、味觉、感觉和视觉。当时我害怕我眼中看见的所有东西。就像孩子找父亲一样，我想向您求助。我不会对你说话，所以你不懂我想要什么。你从我面前跑开，扔下了我，我却不知道是为了什么。

我感到冷，所以我穿上一件您的上衣走进了漆黑的夜晚。我记得当我从街上走过时，我还在哭。当我走到一片森林时，我太累了，就在一条小溪旁躺了下来。

我睡了几个小时后醒了过来，感到又饥又渴。我喝了些溪水，又在地上找了些野果吃。我在森林中住了一个月，我每天观察天上的太阳和月亮，聆听林中那动听的鸟鸣。我想学鸟叫，但学不会；相反，我只能发出的那难听的吼声，把野兽都吓跑了。后来我开始探索森林

remember: *v.* 记住【搭配】remember doing sth. 记起来做了某事 remember to do sth. 记着要做某事

the beautiful sounds of the birds in the trees. I
tried to make their sounds, but I could not. Instead,
I could only make loud, ugly noises that frightened
the animals. Soon I began to explore the area outside the forest. One night I found a fire that some
people must have made. I liked the warm light, and
I put my hand into the hot fire. Quickly, I pulled it
back with *a cry of pain*. Then, I did not understand
that fire burns you. I did not know why something
that looked good could give so much pain. I stared
at the things the people had used to make the fire.
Soon I learned that they used wood. I found that
nuts and roots tasted better if I cooked them in the
fire before eating them. But fruits did not. Soon, I
could not find any more food, and I knew I had to
leave the forest. When I left the forest I found that
there was a cold, white substance on the ground.
This was snow, of course, but I did not know that
yet. I only knew that it hurt my feet and made them
cold. I walked for three days without food or sleep.
One morning, I found a small house. I was so hungry and tired that I opened the door and went into

之外的世界。一天夜里我找到了一堆人用过的火。我喜欢那温暖的火光，就把手伸进了火里。但我立刻痛得叫了一声并缩回了手。当时我不明白火会烧伤人。我也不明白为什么看上去美好的东西却给人带来的却是痛苦。我盯着人们用来生火的东西，很快我就明白他们用的是木头。我发现坚果和块根在吃以前先在火上烧熟味道会更美，但水果则不然。可很快我便找不到其他吃的东西了，于是我明白自己必须要离开这片森林。我离开森林时，发现地上有一种冰冷的、白色的物质。这当然是雪了，但我当时还不知道，只知道它使我的脚冰凉难受。我不吃不睡地走了三天。有一天早晨，我发现一座小房子。我饿坏了，也累坏了，马上推门走了进去。一个老头儿正坐在火边做饭。他一看见我，就立刻高声叫着跑了出去。我吃了他的饭，躺在他的床上睡着了。

a cry of pain: 一声痛苦的大叫

the house immediately. An old man was sitting by a fire, cooking something. When he saw me, he ran out of the house, screaming loudly. I ate the man's food, then lay down on his bed and fell asleep.

When I woke up it was the middle of the day. I took some of the man's food and left the house. I did not want the man to be hungry, so I only took a little food.

After some hours of walking, I found a small village. I was interested in the nice looking houses, and the gardens with vegetables and fruit trees. I entered one of the houses, and when the women and children saw me, they ran away screaming, just like the old man I had seen in the morning. Soon everyone in the village heard the screams, and men ran out of their houses. They began to throw rocks and shout things at me. I did not understand what they said, but the stones hurt me and I knew the people were angry. Quickly I ran away from the village. In the evening, I found a small house that had a very small wooden building *attached* to it. I did not want to enter the house, because I knew the

我一直睡到中午才醒过来，拿了一些那个人的食物就离开了。我不想让那个人挨饿，所以我只取了一点食物。

　　走了数小时后，我发现了一个小村庄。我对那些漂亮的房子、菜园和果园很感兴趣。我走进一户人家，那家的女人们和孩子们一见到我，就像我早晨见到的那个老头儿一样，尖叫着跑了出去。很快全村人都听到了她们的叫声。男人们都跑了出来。他们一面向我投石块一面冲我大喊大叫。我不懂他们在说什么，但石头打得我很疼，我知道他们发怒了，我就赶快从村子里跑了出去。傍晚时，我找到了一座小房子，和房子相连的还有一个小小的木屋。我不想进入房子里，因为我知道人们会害怕而且可能会伤害我；然而，我还是走进了那小小的木屋。它太小了，我根本无法站直。因为我个子太高，只能坐在里面。但我并不在意，我已在外面度过好多夜晚了，能有个地方睡觉我已很高兴了。我想在这儿人们找不到我。我找了一些草铺了个床，然后就睡下了。第二天早上我往外看，看到房子旁边有一处养猪的地

attach: v. 附着；与…相连 [搭配] attach to 与…连在一起

people would be afraid and might try to hurt me. However, I did go into the little wooden building. The place was so small that I could not stand up. I could only sit down inside it, because I am so large. But I did not mind. I was happy to have a place to sleep, after being outside for many nights. I also thought that people would not find me here. I found some straw to make a bed, and then fell asleep. The next morning, I looked outside and saw that there was an area for pigs and some water next to the house. I looked at the wall between the wooden building and the house, and I saw that there was a hole in the wall. When I looked through it, I saw a room inside the house. No one was in the room. Quickly and quietly, I left the wooden hut and went into the house. I needed to find something to eat. I found some bread and a cup, which I used to drink some water. I decided to live in the little wood place *until* someone made me leave it. This was much better than living outside, in the cold, dark forest.

The days passed. I learned that a family

方，还有一些水。我看了看木房子和我这小木屋之间的那道墙，发现墙上有个洞。我透过洞往里望，发现里面有一间房，而且房中空无一人。我迅速而悄悄地离开小木屋走进了那房子里，我需要找些吃的。我找到一些面包和一个杯子——我用它喝了点水。我决定在有人赶走我之前就住在这个小木屋里，这比住在外面那寒冷、漆黑的森林中强多了。

　　数天以后，我知道住在这座房子中的人姓

until: prep. 直到。如：Nothing has happened until Friday. 星期五前什么事都未发生（之后出了很多事）。

93

named De Lacey lived in the house. There was a young man named Felix, a pretty girl named Agatha, and their old, blind father. I did not know his name. This family was very poor, and Felix and Agatha had to work very hard to care for their father. Often, they would give their father their own food, so that he could eat. They had only a little milk from an old cow, and a few vegetables from their garden.

Even though they were poor, the family was happy and full of love and kindness. I could not take any more food from them; instead, I wanted to help them. I went out at night and looked for nuts and berries in the forest. I also cut wood for the family, using Felix's tools. When the family found these gifts, they were so happy that I, also, became happy. I *was* very *surprised to see* that the people used fire inside their house. They cooked with it and used it to fill the room with light. At night, Felix and Agatha used the fire's light to read to their blind father. The words they read were just like the words they spoke. I soon learned that they used

德拉西。一个年轻男子叫费利克斯，一个漂亮姑娘叫阿加莎，还有他们那年老的双目失明的父亲，可我并不知道他的名字。这家人很穷。费利克斯和阿加莎整天劳碌来养活他们的老父亲。他们经常把自己盘中的食物分给老人，好让他多吃一点。他们只有一头产奶量不多的老奶牛，菜园中只有几种蔬菜。

这家人尽管穷，却非常幸福，充满了关爱和友善。我不忍心再取他们的食物，相反我想帮助他们。我晚上出去，到森林里寻找坚果和浆果，我也用费利克斯的工具为这家人砍柴。当他们发现这些礼物时，他们很高兴，而我也感到高兴。我吃惊地看到人们在屋内也使用火。他们用它做饭，也用它照明。晚上，费利克斯和阿加莎借助火光给他们的盲父读书。他们念的字和他们说话用的字是一样的。我很快就明白了他们读的东西叫做"书"。几个月过去了，我不断学说他们所说的语言。我极想和这些善良的人说话，也许他们不在意我长得有多吓人……噢，是的，弗兰肯斯坦博士，我已经知道了我有多丑，有一天我在他们家旁边的池塘里看到了我的面孔。我突然明白为什么人人都怕我了。一天上午，一个长着黑色长发的美丽姑娘来到了这座房子里。费利克斯高兴

be surprised to see sth.: 惊诧于看到某物

things called "books" to read with. As the
months passed, I taught myself to say their words. I
wanted deeply to talk to these kind people. Maybe
they would not mind how horrible I looked... Oh,
yes, Dr. Frankenstein, I had learned just how ugly I
was. I had seen my face in the water of the pond
next to the family's house one day. Suddenly, I understood why everyone was afraid of me. One morning, a beautiful girl with long black hair came to
the house. Felix greeted her happily, and I learned
her name was Safie. Safie had come from a country
called Turkey, and did not speak the same language as the De Lacey family. She was going to
marry Felix. After Safie came, the family spent
many hours teaching her to speak and read their
language. Through the holes in the wall, I listened
to them talk and learned to speak many of their
words.

One day, when I was walking in the forest
looking for fruits, I found a box that had some old
books inside it. I used those books to teach myself
to read.

地欢迎她，我得知她的名字叫萨菲。萨菲来自一个叫土耳其的国家，她说的语言和德拉西一家人的语言不同。她就要嫁给费利克斯了。萨菲来了以后，这家人花费了很多时间教她讲和读他们的语言。透过墙上的那个洞，我能听到他们说话，也学会了许多他们的话。

　　一天，当我在森林里漫步寻找野果时发现了一个箱子，里面有一些旧书。我拿这些书自己学着阅读。

I spent the winter and spring months happily. I was *enjoying* my simple life, and quietly watching the happy family. Because I had lived with them for so long and done things to help them, I felt connected to them, even if they did not know I was there. I was quickly learning to read and speak their language, too. But what good were these words, when I had no one to speak them with? Would I ever have friends? Would anyone ever look at me with love in his or her eyes? I did not think so. Even you, Victor Frankenstein ran away from me, and I thought of you as my father. As I thought about my lonely life more, I began to feel angry towards you.

You will remember I told you that on the first night of my life, I took one of your coats with me when I left your house. I found your notebook in the coat pocket. At first, I did not understand the words inside the notebook, because I could not read. But after I learned to read, I read all about your work and your thoughts before you began to create me. I learned how frightened you were when

整个冬季和春季我过得非常愉快。我喜欢我那简单的生活，也喜欢看着这幸福的一家人。由于我和他们在一起生活了这么长时间，还为他们做了许多事；即使他们不知道我的存在，我也觉得和他们连在一起了。我也正迅速地学会阅读他们的书籍和讲他们的语言。但没有人和我说话，我学这些又有什么用呢？我会有朋友吗？会有人眼中含有爱意地去看我一眼吗？我可不这样想。即使你，维克多·弗兰肯斯坦，虽然我把你看作是父亲，你还是从我的面前跑开了。我对我这种孤独无依的生活想得越多，我越开始生你的气。

你要记住，我告诉过你，你赐予我生命的那天晚上，我离开你的住处时，穿上了你的一件上衣。上衣口袋里有你的笔记本。开始因为我不识字，我不懂里面的话。但我学会识字后，我看了你在创造我以前所做的一切事情和你的想法。我明白当你第一次看到我那丑陋的身躯时，你有多么恐惧。

enjoy: *v.* 从…中获得乐趣 [搭配] enjoy sth./doing sth. 喜欢做某事 [习语] enjoy oneself 感到快乐，愉快

99

you saw my ugly body for the first time.

Frankenstein, why did you make me so ugly that even you hated me, and were afraid of me? Because of the way I look, I have always been alone. I hated the day you gave me life, and I hated you.

But when I thought of the kind family I watched, I did not feel so angry. I deeply wanted to believe that they would become my friends when I told them my story. They would not be afraid of my size or my face.

But even though I wanted to talk to them, a part of me did not want to show my face to them. I was afraid that they would run away in fear. By this time, I had lived in the little wooden house for one year. Finally, I decided to try and meet the family. I decided to try and enter their house when Felix, Agatha, and Safie were away. The old blind man would be alone. Since he could not see me, he probably would not be afraid of me. When the others came back, they would see that their father liked me. Maybe then, they would like me too. One

弗兰肯斯坦,你为什么把我造得这样丑陋,竟然连你都讨厌我、都害怕我呢?由于我的长相,我一直孤苦伶仃。我痛恨你赐予我生命的那一天,我也恨你。

但当我想起我看到的那家好心人时,我又不觉得那么气愤了。我衷心地希望他们听了我的遭遇后会成为我的朋友,我相信他们是不会害怕我的身材和我的面孔的。

但即便我想和他们谈话,我也不希望让他们看到我的面孔。我怕他们会被我吓跑。当我在那小木屋中已住了快一年时,最终我决定试着去和他们见面。我决定趁费利克斯、阿加莎和萨菲不在时试着走进去。那个瞎眼老头儿一个人在家,既然他看不见,他可能不会怕我。等其他人回来时,他们会看到他们的父亲喜欢我,也许那时候他们也会喜欢我的。一天早晨,年轻人都到村里去了,我知道我的机会来了。我离开小木屋,走到他们的门前敲门。我极担心以后会发生什么事。但德拉西喊了声"请进。"我深吸一口气,推开了门。我说我是一个赶路的人,需要休息,并问他我能否呆在这儿和他说会儿话。老人善意地给了我点吃的

***agree:** v.*同意;(意见)一致 [搭配] agree about sb./sth. with sb. 在某人/某事上与某人达成一致 agree to sth. 同意某事

101

morning the young people went to the village. I
knew that now was my chance. I left the little
wooden house, walked up to their door, and
knocked. I was terribly afraid of what would happen
next. De Lacey called, "Come in." I took a deep
breath and opened the door. I told him that I was a
traveler who needed rest, and asked if I could stay
and talk to him. The old man kindly gave me a little food and told me to sit with him. We spent the
day talking about many things. We agreed that a
man's friends are more important than anything. I
really believed that De Lacey's kind words meant
that had become my friend. I fell on my knees and
held his hand, when the door opened suddenly. The
horrible things that happened next are still painful
for me to remember. The young people saw me, and
Safie ran out of the door, screaming. Agatha turned
white and fell to the ground. Felix jumped at me
and pulled me away from his father. "Oh, God!
What are you?" he shouted. "Father, I will save
you from this horrible monster!" I fell to the floor
as Felix began hitting me with a stick. I could have

并请我和他坐在一起。我们谈了一天，谈了许多事情。我们都认为友谊是最重要的。我真心相信德拉西那善良的话意味着他已经成了我的朋友。我跪下来握住了他的手，门突然开了。后面发生的可怕事情让我至今想起来都痛苦不堪。年轻人看到了我。萨菲尖叫着跑了出去；阿加莎脸色苍白，倒在地上；费利克斯跳过来把我从他父亲身边拖开。"噢，上帝，你是个什么东西？"他吼道，"父亲，我要把你从这可怕的怪物手中救出来！"费利克斯开始用一根木棒打我，我倒在了地上。我可以轻易地杀死他，但我没有动手。我以最快的速度跑出了这座房子。我比你所能想象的还难过。

killed him easily, but I did not. I ran away from their house as fast as I could. I was unhappier than you can imagine.

I was alone in the world once again. I had no friends; I would never have any friends. My anger was terrible to see. I did not want love anymore; I wanted only *revenge* on the world that had hurt me. And I wanted to find you, Frankenstein. I promised myself that I would make you suffer.

弗兰肯斯坦

　　我在这个世界上又孤独无依了，我没有朋友，我永远也不会有朋友。我怒气冲天，我不再想得到爱了；因为这个世界伤害了我，我只想复仇。弗兰肯斯坦，我想找到你，我发誓我要让你遭受苦难。

revenge: n. 复仇 take a revenge on sb. for sth. 就某事而向某人复仇

105

CHAPTER THIRTEEN
A Confession

I began to look for you. I knew that you lived in a place called Geneva, because I had listened to the geography lessons that Felix *taught* Safie. I knew which way I had to travel to find the city.

You understand, Frankenstein, that at this time my heart was filled with hate. You gave me a body, a mind, and feelings. Then you left me alone in the world to be feared and hated by everyone, and I know that you hate me the most of all. I truly believed you were evil, and I still think God will punish you for the terrible thing you have done to me.

I traveled in the dark so no one would see me. It was winter, and often snow fell. But I almost never stopped to rest. I thought of nothing but finding you. When I reached the edge of Switzerland, it was springtime. I decided to enjoy the warm, sunny

第十三章
坦白

我开始寻找你。我知道你住在一个叫日内瓦的地方，因为我曾听过费利克斯给萨菲上的地理课。我知道我必须走哪条路才能找到那座城市。

你明白，弗兰肯斯坦，这时我心中全都是仇恨。你给了我身体、头脑和感情。然后你把我丢在这个世界上，孤独无依、人见人怕、人见人恨；而且我知道你是最恨我的人。千真万确，我相信你是个邪恶的人，我现在还认为上帝将会因为你在我身上所犯下的恶行来惩罚你。

为了不让人看到我，我只在晚上赶路。当时是严冬，经常下雪，但我几乎没停下来休息过。我什么也不想，只想找到你。我到达瑞士边境时，已是春天了。我决定享受温暖、明媚的阳光，白天赶路。但为了不让人看见我，我决心穿越森林。然而有一天，我来到了一条小

teach: v. 教；授 teach sb. sth. 教给某人某事

days and travel during the daytime. But I would *make sure to* travel through the forest, so no one would see me. However, one day I reached a river. Suddenly I heard voices near me. I hid behind a tree and watched a little girl run by me. She was laughing, and I thought she was playing a game with someone behind her. Suddenly, she fell into the river.

The strength of the flowing water quickly pulled her away from the edge. I knew I had to save her, or she would die. I jumped in and swam to her. I carried the *unconscious* girl to shore, and she was just waking up, when her father grabbed her from me and ran away. I started to follow them, trying to talk to him. But suddenly he pointed a gun at me and shot! I fell to the ground, crying out in pain.

I had saved the child's life, and this was my reward! Now, I hated the world even more. I had to spend the next few weeks in the forest, resting and *healing* myself. Finally, I was able to continue traveling.

河边时，突然听到附近有声音。我藏在一棵树后，看到一个小姑娘从我身边跑过。她正在笑着。我想她是在和后面的某个人嬉戏，但她突然掉进了河里。

水流的冲击力把她冲离了河岸，我知道我必须救她，否则她会淹死的。我跳进水中游到她身旁。我将这失去知觉的姑娘抱上了岸。就在她快要醒来时，突然她父亲从我手中夺过她转身就跑。我开始跟着他们并试着和他说话，但他突然把一支枪对准了我并开了一枪。我倒在了地上，痛苦地叫着。

我救了那个孩子的命，而这就是我得到的回报！现在，我更加痛恨这个世界。我不得不在森林里休养了几个星期，最终，我又能继续赶路了。

make sure to do sth.: 决心干某事 make sure of sth.: 确定

unconscious: *adj.* 无意识的（昏厥的）；未发现的 [固定用法] be unconscious of sth. 意识到某事

heal: *v.* 治愈 [搭配] heal over/up

Two months later, I reached the forest outside of the city of Geneva. I was tired and hungry, and had just sat down under a tree. I was thinking about how I would find you, and what I would say to you. Suddenly a little boy came running towards me. For a moment, I felt some hope. Here was a child, who probably was not afraid of ugly people, like adults were. Maybe he could be my friend. As the boy ran past me I reached out and grabbed him. He covered his face with his hands and screamed. I did not want him to scream, because others might hear him. I said gently, "I'm not going to hurt you."

"A monster!" he screamed. "Let me go! My father is an important man, and if you hurt me he'll find you and hurt you, too! His name is Alphonse Frankenstein..."

"Frankenstein?" I screamed. "You come from the family of my enemy. Now, I will have my revenge. I will kill you to punish HIM." The child continued to fight and scream terrible things at me. I grabbed his throat and *squeezed* it. In a moment

两个月后，我到了日内瓦城外的森林。我又累又饿，在一棵树下坐了下来。我考虑怎样去找到你，对你说些什么。突然，一个小男孩冲我跑来。我一度觉得有点希望。这是个小孩，他也许不像大人那样害怕丑陋的人。当那个小孩从我身边跑过时，我伸出手抓住了他。他双手捂着脸尖叫起来。我不想让他叫，因为别人可能会听见。我温和地说，"我不会伤害你的。"

　　"怪物！"他大叫起来。"放开我！我父亲可是个大人物。如果你伤了我，他会找到你，饶不了你！他叫阿尔封斯·弗兰肯斯坦……"

　　"弗兰肯斯坦？"我喝道。"你是我仇敌的家人！现在，我要复仇了，我要杀了你去惩罚他！"那个男孩继续和我打斗并朝我喊着可怕的话……我抓住他的咽喉捏了一下，他的脖子就断了，他立马就死了。我意识到我杀了一个无辜的人，吓得瘫倒在地。我看着地上的孩子

squeeze: *v.* 挤，压

111

he was dead, his neck broken. I realized that I had killed an innocent person, and I fell to the ground in horror. I cried as I looked at the little child on the ground. But I knew that this would make you feel great pain, and in a moment, I was glad that I had killed him! As I stared at the dead boy, I saw a necklace around his neck. I picked it up and went closer to the city of Geneva. Soon, I came to a barn. I saw a young woman sleeping there. I wanted to wake her up, but I knew she would only scream. Later, she might remember me, and learn that I was the boy's killer. Even though I did not know what she would do, I decided to make her suffer *anyway*. I put the necklace in the pocket of her dress. Of course, I knew that when it was found, everyone would believe that she was the killer.

When I had done this, I waited until the boy's body was found. Then, when no one was watching, I followed everyone into the city.

I began walking through Geneva, and through these mountains near the city. I knew that one day I would find you. I have waited for this moment for a long time. And now, at last, it is here!

哭了起来。但我马上想到这会让你极度痛苦，因此我很高兴杀死了他。我盯着他的尸体，看到他脖子上有一条项链。我摘下项链向日内瓦城走去。不久，我来到了一个谷仓，看到一个年轻女子正在里面睡觉。我想叫醒她，但我知道她只会大叫。以后她会记住我并明白我是杀害那个孩子的凶手。虽然不知道看见我后她到底会怎么做，但我决定无论如何都要让她受苦。我把项链放进她的口袋。我当然知道项链一旦被人发现，人人都会相信她就是凶手。

做完这一切后，我一直等到有人找到了那男孩的尸体后，才趁人不备，尾随众人进了城。

我开始穿越日内瓦城，穿越城市附近的群山去寻找你。我知道总有一天我会找到你的。这一刻我已等了很久了。现在终于在这儿找到了你！

anyway: adv. 无论如何；至少（= anyhow）。如：It is too late, anyway. 不管怎样，这都是迟了。

113

CHAPTER FOURTEEN
The Promise

The monster stopped talking and looked at me, waiting for me to say something.

I did not know what to think. I was still *angry with* him, but as I listened to his story, I had also felt pity, because of the cruel way everyone had treated him. I felt that I should help him in some way. I looked into his yellow eyes and said, "All right, monster. I have talked with you, and I feel sorry for you. What do you want me to do?" "I want you to make me a friend. One who will not be afraid of my ugly face and body. One who will understand me, and like me. I want you to create that friend... a woman! Make a wife for me." When I thought about a woman monster, I felt sick inside. I shouted *in* anger, "Never! I will not create another thing like you, and then watch it do the same terrible things you have done! Kill me if you want, but I will not do this!" "Frankenstein, listen to

114

第十四章
誓言

怪物停下来看着我，等着我说话。

我不知该做何想。我还在生他的气，但我听了他的遭遇，又觉得他好可怜，因为所有人都用这种残暴的方式对待他。我觉得我该在某些方面帮助他。我盯着他的黄眼睛说，"好吧，怪物，我已和你谈过，也为你感到遗憾。你想让我为你做点什么呢？""我想让你给我造一个朋友，一个不怕我那丑陋的脸孔和身体的人，一个理解我并喜欢我的人。我想让你造的那个朋友……是一个女人。为我造一个妻子。"当我想到那是一个女怪物时，我顿时觉得恶心。我怒喝道，"休想！我不会再创造一个像你一样的东西，然后看着它像你一样做出恶行！你想杀我可以，但我绝不做这件事。""弗兰肯斯坦，听我说，"他温和地说。"我曾尽力去爱人类，但所有的人都像你一样恨我。如果你肯给我一点理解和慈悲的话，我便不会再打扰你了。""不！造出你以后，我一病数月。我不会再这么做的！这太可怕了，你怎么敢说这样的话？"

angry: *adj.* 愤怒的，生气的
[搭配] be angry with sb. 对某人发脾气

me," he said quietly. "I have tried to love people, but all anyone has done is hate me, just as you have. If you can treat me with understanding and a little kindness, I will leave you alone." "No! I was sick for many months after I made you. I won't do this again! It is too horrible! How dare you say these things?"

The monster stood up. "*Selfish coward*! If you don't do what I ask, I will destroy everything you love. I will destroy your whole life!" These words made me think. If I did not make a friend for the monster, he might try to hurt my family again. And, in my heart, I knew that I *owed* the monster something. Because of me, he had lived a life of pain and loneliness.

Seeing that I was thinking quietly, the monster said, "Frankenstein, if you make this woman for me, no one will see either of us again. We will go far away from here, to some country full of forests where there are no people. We will never hurt men or animals." These words made my heart sad for the being I had created. But when I turned to look

怪物站起身来。"自私的懦夫！你要是不按我的要求去做，我会毁掉你所爱的一切，我会毁掉你的一生。"这些话让我不得不去想一下后果。如果我不给这怪物造出一个朋友，他可能又会试图去伤害我的亲人。而且在我的心里，我知道我欠他一些东西，正是因为我，他才会生活在痛苦与孤独之中。

怪物看到我在沉思，就说，"弗兰肯斯坦，如果你为我造出这个女人，谁也不会再见到我们的。我们会远离此地，到某个到处是森林的国度，在那儿没有一个人。我们绝不会伤害任何人或任何动物。"这些话让我为这个我创造出的家伙感到难过。但当我转头看他时，我看到的只是杀我弟弟的凶手。但是我也知道，只有做了他要求的事，我才能保护我的亲人和我自己。我已经见过这个怪物一旦发起怒

selfish: *adj.* 自私的 selfish-ness: *n.* 自私

coward: *n.* 胆小鬼 cowardice: *n.* 胆小；胆怯

owe: *v.* 欠 [搭配] owe sb. sth. 或 owe sth. to sb. 欠某人某物

117

at him, all I saw was the killer of my brother. But I knew that by doing what he wanted, I would protect my family and myself. I had seen that when the monster was angry, he could do terrible things. Finally I said, "I will do what you want. But you must promise me that as soon as I have made this monster woman, you will leave Europe forever. If you don't... I will kill you." The monster stared at me and did not say anything for a minute. "How would you kill me, Victor Frankenstein? I am much stronger than you... but I promise you that you will never see me again, if you do what I want. Thank you! Now, begin this work immediately. I will be watching you all the time, and when I see that you are done, I will come and meet my wife." Before I could say anything, the monster left the *shelter*. I watched him walk down the mountain. Soon, he had disappeared. It was evening when I left the mountain. I was crying bitterly, and I hated myself again. -But I would do this terrible thing.

That day I went to Geneva. I had to begin my work as soon as possible.

来，就会做出疯狂的事。最后我说，"我按你的要求去做，但你必须发誓，我一旦给你造出那个女怪物来，你就得永远地离开欧洲。否则……我会杀掉你的。"怪物盯着我看了一会儿，什么话也没有说。"你怎样杀死我，维克多·弗兰肯斯坦？我比你强壮得多……但我发誓，一旦你如我所愿，你绝不会再见到我。谢谢您！现在你要马上开始，我会一直监视你。当我看到你的工作完成时，我会来见我的妻子的。"我还未来得及说话，怪物已走出了木屋。我看着他走下山，很快就消失了。我离开山顶时已是傍晚。我痛哭不止，转而又痛恨自己。但我还是要去做这件事。

那天我回到了日内瓦，我必须尽快开始工作。

shelter: *n.* 庇护；遮蔽 a shelter from rain 避雨的地方

119

CHAPTER FIFTEEN
The Second Monster

My family was very worried when they saw me, and they were frightened that I would not answer any of their questions. I could not tell them anything. I had to leave them immediately to save them from the monster. But weeks went by, and I could not find enough courage to begin to build the second monster. The thought of the work gave me bad dreams. I knew the monster would do something terrible if I *broke my promise*, but I also knew that the job would take time. I had to study for many months before I could even begin. During these weeks, my health became better, and my father was very happy. One day he said to me, " Victor, it is time to end our sadness over William's death. We must continue our lives, my son. You know your mother and I wanted you and Elizabeth to marry. I hope this will happen one day soon. I am growing older, and I would like to see

第十五章
第二个怪物

家里人看到我后都很忧虑,而我不肯回答他们的问题又令他们恐惧。我无法对他们说什么。为使他们免遭怪物的毒手,我必须马上离开。但几个星期过去了,我却找不到足够的勇气去着手造第二个怪物。想到这种工作我就常做噩梦。我明白如果我毁誓,那个怪物就会做出疯狂的事来,但我也知道做这种事需要时间,工作开始之前我必须先研究数月。在这几周里,我身体状况好转了。父亲非常高兴。一天,他对我说,"维克多,我们该结束对威廉之死的哀痛了。孩子,我们要继续我们的生活。你知道我和你母亲都希望你和伊丽莎白结婚,我希望越早越好。我越来越老,我希望在死前看到你幸福。""父亲,我当然愿娶伊丽莎白,我爱她。"我赶快告诉他。但我也在想我对怪物发过的那个可怕的誓言。我在娶伊丽莎白以前,不得不先给怪物造出一个妻子。这是我们取得幸福的惟一途径。我在家期间,阅读了一些人体实验的报告,这些实验是在英格兰完成的,所以我决定到那儿去进行我的工作。这件可怕的工作必须在远离我所爱的人的地方去做,所以我对父亲说,"父亲,我有些工作必须在英格兰完成。然后,我要做些短途

break one's promise: 毁约

you happy before I die." "Father, of course I want to marry Elizabeth. I love her," " I told him quickly. But I was thinking of the terrible promise I had made to the monster. Before I could marry Elizabeth, I had to create a wife for the monster. It was the only way we could all be happy. While I was at home, I read about some experiments on the human body. These experiments were being done in England, and I decided to go there and do my work. I wanted to do this terrible job very far away from the people I loved. So, I told my father, "Father, I have some work I must finish in England. After that, I would like to travel a little, to become completely calm and healthy. Then I will marry Elizabeth with love and happiness." My father and Elizabeth were happy when they heard my plans. They wanted me to go to England, but because they were still *worried* about me, Elizabeth asked my friend Henry Clerval to travel with me. At the end of September Henry and I left Geneva. We traveled through France, Germany and Holland before arriving in England. I spent four months in

旅行，使自己完全心情平静、身体健康。然后我会充满爱恋和快乐去娶伊丽莎白为妻。"父亲和伊丽莎白听了我的计划都很高兴。他们愿意让我到英格兰去。出于对我的担心，伊丽莎白请我的朋友亨利·克勒瓦尔陪我去。九月底，我和亨利离开了日内瓦，我们途经法国、德国和荷兰到达英格兰。我在英格兰用了四个月时间阅读有关人体的最新信息资料，在此期间，我找全了制造第二个怪物所需要的各种仪器和材料。然后，我和亨利用两个月的时间在苏格兰访友。但当时我知道我应该早几个月就开始这个吓人的工作。我不清楚如果怪物知道我还没有开始给他制造朋友后会发生什么事。他会伤害伊丽莎白和我父亲吗？他在跟踪我和亨利吗？我想象我看到了他那丑陋的黄眼睛在随时随地盯着我们。在那些接不到我父亲和伊丽莎白信件的日子里，我非常害怕。在任何地方我都紧随着亨利，生怕我不在场时那个怪物会伤害他。最终我确定了在何时何地开始我的工作，但首先我要让亨利离开我。我对他说，"我们已经在苏格兰逍遥了一些日子了，但我需要单独呆一段时间，也许一到两个月。你为何不留在这儿呢？我要回英格兰去，等我回来时，我就又成为你原来认识的那个快乐的维克多了。我向你保证，我将成为一个更好的朋友。"亨利大笑起来，他说，"真的，维克多，你知道无论你要去哪儿，我都会陪你去。但你想独处，也是件好事，一定记着早点回来。"我告诉亨利我要去英格兰，但这是句谎话。相

worried: *adj.* 担忧的，担心的 be worried about sth. 就某事担心

123

England reading the new information about the human body. During that time, I found all the tools and materials I needed to build a second monster. After that, Henry and I spent two months visiting friends in Scotland. But by then, I knew that I should have begun my terrible work many months ago. I did not know what would happen if the monster learned that I had not yet started to make his friend. Would he hurt Elizabeth and my father? Was he *following* Henry and me? I imagined I saw his ugly yellow eyes following me everywhere. On the days when no letters came from my father or Elizabeth I was afraid. I followed Henry everywhere, afraid that the monster would hurt him if I weren't with him. Finally, I decided when to start and where I would work. But first, I had to get Henry to leave me. I told him, We've been happy in Scotland for some time now, but I need to be alone for awhile. Maybe a month or two. Why don't you stay here? I'm going back to England, but when I return, I'll be the same happy Victor you used to know. I will be a much better friend, I promise

反，我离开亨利去了奥克尼群岛——那是苏格兰附近的一些小岛。其中一座岛上只有五个居民，我想在那儿进行我的工作。我租了一座又黑又脏的房子。它只有两个房间，而且墙壁极脏，但我并不在乎。我打扫了房子后，把其中一间作为工作室。我终于坐下来开始工作了。

follow: *v.* 跟随，响应；仿效 follow the fashion 赶时髦 follow one's bent 做自己感兴趣的事，随心所欲 follow the crowd 随大流

you." Henry laughed. "Really, Victor," he said, "You know I want to be with you, no matter where you're going. But if you want to be alone, that's fine. Just come back quickly!" I had told Henry I was going to England, but this was a lie. Instead, when I left Henry I went to the Orkney Islands, some small islands near Scotland. One of the islands had only five people living on it, and I wanted to work there. I *rented* a dark, dirty little house. It had two small rooms and dirty paint on the walls, but I did not care. I cleaned the house and made one room into my workroom. Then, I finally sat down to begin my work.

I hated my work more and more as I built the horrible monster woman's body. Sometimes, I could not go into the workroom for days. Other times, I worked day and night and did not eat or sleep. I thought back to the first monster I had made, and remembered how excited I was. Then, I did not know the horror of what I was doing. How stupid I was! I only wanted to become a great scientist. Now, I knew the meaning of what I was doing. I hated the moment for making me build him a friend, but I hated myself even more. Whenever I worked, I looked around me, thinking I would see the monster in front of me every second. I raised my eyes constantly fearing to see the monster appear in front of me...

But the work was going well. I was almost finished with the second monster. I would give the woman life, and both monsters would leave me forever. Why then was I afraid all the time? I had a feeling that something bad was going to happen again.

我制造那个可怕的女怪物身体的同时，对这件工作却越来越痛恨。有时候，我一连几天都没法走进工作室，但有时我却废寝忘食、夜以继日地工作。回想起我造的第一个怪物，当时我是那么兴奋，因为当时我还不知道我做的事情有多恐怖。当时我太蠢了，只想成为一个伟大的科学家。现在我知道了做这件事的意义，我恨那怪物强迫我给他造一个朋友，但我更恨我自己。每当我工作时，我都东张西望，认为我随时都能看到那个怪物出现在眼前。我不断抬起头来，惟恐看到那个怪物在我面前突

rent: *v.* rent sth. (out) to sb. at sth. 以某代价将某物租给某人 *n.* 出租

127

hated the monster for making me build him a friend, but I hated myself even more. Whenever I worked, I looked around me, thinking I would see the monster in front of me every second. I raised my eyes *constantly*, fearing to see the monster appear in front of me.

But the work was going well. I was almost finished with the second monster. I would give the woman life, and both monsters would leave me forever. Why, then, was I afraid all the time? I had a feeling that something bad was going to happen again.

然现身。

　　但工作进展顺利，第二个怪物已基本完成。我将给予其生命，然后两个怪物将永远离开我。那么，我为什么总是害怕呢？我有种预感——还会有坏事发生。

---

constantly: *adv*. 经常地；总是

CHAPTER SIXTEEN
The Monster's Threat

O ne night as I sat in my workroom I realized that I had no idea what kind of *character* the new monster would have. I thought, "When I built the first monster, I didn't know he was going to be so angry and terrible! I do not know what this new monster will be like! What if she is more awful than her husband? What if she wants to kill people? What if she does not want to go to another country? If the monsters don't like each other, will I have to build another one?" But then an even more *horrifying* thought came to me. "What if the monsters do like each other, and go to another country... and have children? Then the children could destroy more people! " In those moments, I believed that my promise to the monster had been a terrible mistake. Everything that happened would be terrible! Suddenly, I looked up and saw the monster's face at the window! He was

第十六章
怪物的威胁

一天晚上，我坐在工作间时突然意识到，我一点也不了解这个新怪物会有一种什么性格。我想，"当我制造第一个怪物时，我可不知道他会是如此暴躁而且可怕！我不知这个新的怪物又会如何！她要是比丈夫更可怕怎么办？她要是想杀人怎么办？她要是不想到别的国家去可怎么办？如果这两个怪物不和，我是否还得再造出一个来呢？"但接着我又有了一个更可怕的念头。"如果这两个怪物确实十分恩爱，也去了别的国家……而且生下了孩子可怎么办？然后那些孩子们可能会毁灭更多的人"。当时，我确信我对怪物的承诺已经铸成了大错。任何事情发生都将极为可怕！突然，我抬起头来，看到怪物的脸出现在窗外。他正盯着看他那未来的妻子，他那大黑嘴巴上露出一丝狞笑。

character: n. 性格

horrifying: *adj.* 可怕的 horri-

fy: *vt.* 吓唬

131

staring at his new wife, and an ugly smile moved his black mouth.

When I saw that smile, I thought he was planning to do some new awful thing. I had been stupid to try to help him!

Immediately I grabbed the female monster's body and began to tear it into pieces. Legs, arms, and other body parts fell onto the floor of the workroom. I looked at the monster in the window one more time before I ran out the workroom. The monster shouted angrily. Then he disappeared into the night! For the next few hours I sat in the other room, staring at the sea. I was trying not to think about what would happen next. The moon was large and bright, and I heard the voices of fishermen on the water. What was the monster doing? Suddenly, I saw a boat coming quickly towards the shore. When it arrived, I saw the monster jump out of the boat and walk up the path to my house.

I wanted to run, but I could not move. I knew that I should not have destroyed the monster's friend. Now, he would kill me.

我一看到那丝笑容，就认为他在计划着某种新的恶行。我试图帮助他真是太蠢了！

我立即抓住那女怪物的身体并开始将之撕成碎片。腿、胳膊和身体的其他部分散落在工作室里。我从工作室跑出来以前又看了那怪物一眼。他愤怒地大叫，然后消失在黑夜中。此后的几个小时里，我坐在另一间屋里，凝视着大海。我试图不去想以后会发生什么事。月亮大大的，明晃晃的，海上传来渔夫们说话的声音。那个怪物在干什么呢？我突然看到一只小船飞快地向岸边行来，船一到岸。我就看见那怪物跳出小船向我的住处奔来。

我想跑开，但却动弹不得。我知道我不该毁了怪物的朋友。现在，他要杀我了。

I began to tremble again, knowing that the monster was coming. I wanted to run, but I *was frozen to* my chair.

Moments later, the door opened and the monster came in. "Why did you break your promise, Frankenstein?" he cried. "Why did you destroy my hopes after all this time?" I could not look at him. "Leave me alone!" I screamed. "I broke my promise because I cannot make another thing as ugly and evil as you are; a monster who will kill innocent people!" The monster stared at my red face. He spoke quietly, but his words were like a knife in my heart. "I promised you that if you made me a friend, I would leave you in peace. I would never kill another human being; I did not want to kill anyone. I would never *lie* to you, but you have lied to me. You call me evil? Yes, I am evil... now. And I am more powerful than you, Frankenstein, my creator."

I was too angry to be afraid. "Yes, you are more powerful than me, but I'm not afraid of you!" I yelled, waving a knife in the air. His yellow eyes

知道怪物要来，我又开始颤抖。我想逃走，但却呆在椅子上无法动弹。

一会儿，门开了。怪物走了进来。"你为什么违背诺言，弗兰肯斯坦？"他高叫着。"过了这么长时间了，你为什么要毁掉我的希望呢？"我无法正视他，只是叫道，"滚开！我违背诺言是因为我不能再造出一个像你一样又丑又邪恶的东西，一个滥杀无辜的怪物！"那个怪物盯着我涨红的脸，轻轻地说了几句话，但这些话就像一把刀一样扎在我的心头。"我向你发过誓，如果你给我造出一个朋友，我会让你平静生活；我不会再杀一人，我一个人也不想杀。我绝不会对你说谎。你说我是恶人？是的，我现在……就是恶人。我比你强大，弗兰肯斯坦，你这个创造我的人。"

我勃然大怒，忘记了害怕。"是的，你比我强大，但我并不怕你！"我边喊边挥舞着一把刀子。他的黄眼睛几乎要喷出火来。他说，

be frozen to sth.: 呆在某处不动
lie: v.说谎 lie in one's teeth 撒下弥天大谎

burned with fire. He said, "As long as I live, you will be miserable. I will have my revenge on you! This is my only reason for living!" "Get out! Get out, you evil thing!" I screamed. Now the monster had evil in his voice. "Yes... I am evil. But you are more evil than I, because of what you have done! I'll go. But remember, I'll always be with you. I'll be with you... on the night of your marriage to sweet Elizabeth! Won't she be sad?" And he laughed a horrible laugh. I jumped at him, trying to cut him with the knife. But he was too quick, and ran out of the house. Moments later he was in his boat and moving across the water. I stood on the edge of the water, hearing the monster's words again in my head. I was filled with anger as I heard his words again in my mind. "I will be with you on your *wedding night.*"

So he was going to kill me on my wedding night. I was not afraid for myself, but I couldn't bring this pain and fear to Elizabeth. She truly loved me... tears fell down my face. I told myself I would not let the monster kill me without a long and terrible fight.

"只要我还活着，你就要过凄惨的生活。我要向你复仇！而这就是我还活着的惟一原因。" "滚出去！滚出去，你这恶毒的东西！"我高叫着。现在怪物的声音变得邪恶起来。"是的……我恶毒，但你做的事比我还要恶毒！我走了，但你记住，我会一直跟着你。在你和美丽的伊丽莎白的新婚之夜……我会到场的！难道她会不难过吗？"他发出一阵可怕的大笑。我向他扑过去，试图用手中的刀去砍他。但他动作太快了，一下子就跑了出去。一会儿他就上了船顺流而去。我站在岸边，脑子里想着怪物的话。当我再想起他的话时，"在你的新婚之夜我会到场的。"我简直怒不可遏。

这就是说，他要在我新婚之夜杀死我。我并不为自己害怕，但我却不能把痛苦和恐惧带给伊丽莎白。她确实爱我……泪水顺着我的脸庞滚滚而下。我对自己说我要和他进行长期的激烈搏斗，绝不会让他轻易杀死我。

wedding night: 新婚之夜

CHAPTER SEVENTEEN
More Deaths and Sadness

T he next morning I left the island to find Henry. I knew he wanted to see me and continue traveling. We had planned to go to more places in Europe together before I married Elizabeth. So, after washing and *packing* away all my instruments, I gathered the body parts of the second monster and put them in a large box. Looking at the body parts made me sick. Then, I put some large rocks in the box to make it sink into the water. I stayed in the small house until night came, and then put the box in a little boat. I took the boat a few miles away from the land, and then threw it into the water when a cloud hid the moon.

As the box sank into the water, I felt a little better. At least no one would ever know what I had done on the island. Soon, the beautiful night and the gentle moving of the boat in the water made me fall asleep.

第十七章
更多的死亡与痛苦

第二天一早，我决定离岛去找亨利。我知道他想见到我并继续旅行。我们已经计划好在我结婚之前，一起到欧洲更多的地方。因此，洗漱后，我把所有的仪器打包收拾好，把第二个怪物的身体部件收集起来装进了一个大箱子。看到这些零碎肢体就让我恶心。接着我又往箱子里放了一些大石头以便让其沉入水底。我在那座小房子里一直等到天黑，然后把箱子放到小船上。我将船划到离岛几英里远的地方，然后趁乌云遮住月亮时将箱子扔进了水中。

箱子沉入水中后，我感觉好了一点。至少没人知道我在岛上干了些什么。不久，美好的夜色和海水轻柔的荡漾将我带入了梦乡。

pack: *v.*收拾；将某物装入某物中 pack the clothes into the trunk 将衣服装入衣箱中 pack sth. away （因长久不用而）将某物收拾进柜中

I slept for many hours. When I woke up, it was late in the morning.

A strong wind was blowing. I realized that while I was sleeping, the wind had taken my boat far out into the Atlantic Ocean, away from land. I did not know where I was! Hours passed and I became very hungry and *thirsty*. I knew that if I did not find land, I could drown, or starve to death. As it got dark, I saw some land to the south. Quickly, I traveled towards the lights I saw in the distance. When I put the boat onto the beach, some people came up to me and stared at me. They did not ask to help me, which was surprising. I was dirty, tired, and hungry. They only looked at me and talked to each other. I did not understand their actions, but I asked them, "Friends, could you tell me where I am?"

The people said nothing to me, only stared at me angrily. "What is wrong here? I did not expect English people to treat strangers in this way," I told them. "I don't know anything about how the English treat strangers," said one man. "And I

我睡了很久。等我醒来时，已经快到中午了。

海上正在刮大风。我意识到在我睡觉时，风已把我的小船吹进了大西洋深处。我竟不知身在何处！几个小时过后，我感到饥渴难耐。我知道如果找不到陆地，我就会淹死或饿死。天快黑时，我发现南方有陆地，急忙把船朝远处的灯光处划去。我的小船靠岸时，有些人走上前来目不转睛地看着我。他们并不说要帮助我。这很令人震惊。我又脏、又累、又饿。他们只是看着我，彼此却在说什么。我搞不懂他们的所作所为，但还是问道，"朋友们，能告诉我我是在什么地方吗？"

那些人一言不发，只是愤怒地瞪着我。"这里出什么事了？我倒没想到英国人是如此对待陌生人的。"我对他们说。"我不知道英国人怎样对待陌生人，"一个人说道，"我也不关心这个。你现在是在爱尔兰，而爱尔兰人痛恨罪犯！""罪犯？你什么意思？我没做过

thirsty: *adj.* 渴的 be thirsty for sth. 渴求某物。如：The team is thirsty for success. 这个队渴望胜利。

don't care. You're in Ireland now, and we Irish hate criminals!" "Criminals? What do you mean? I haven't done anything wrong!" I cried. "Well, I don't know about that! You'd better come with me to see Mr. Kirwin, the leader of our town. A man was killed here last night, and he will want to talk to you!" I was upset and angry, but I knew I could make them see that I hadn't killed anyone. I followed the people to Mr. Kirwin's house. The town's leader was a kindly old man, who asked the fisherman to tell their story before letting me talk.

The fisherman said, "Well, sir, I was out in my boat last night, and when the wind began to blow we went back to the land. When we were arriving, I *saw* something *floating* in the water. By the light of the moon, I saw that it was the body of a young man. His body was still warm, and I didn't know if he was dead or unconscious. I dragged him to the beach and tried to wake him up, but it was too late. He was dead.

"At first, I thought that the poor man had drowned in the water. But then I saw the black

任何错事!"我叫道。"嗯，我不知道你有没有做过错事，但你最好和我一起去见我们的市长科文先生。昨晚这里有人被杀。市长会想和你谈谈。"我又急又怒，但我明白我可以让他们相信我没有杀过人。我随着人们来到了科文先生家里。市长是一个和善的老人，在让我讲话前先让那个渔夫讲了他们所见到的事。

渔夫说，"噢，先生，我昨天乘船出海了。开始刮风时，我们返回了陆地。快上岸时，我见到海上漂着什么东西。借着月光，我看到那是一具年轻人的尸体。尸体尚温，我不知他已经死了还是仅仅失去了知觉。我把他拖上岸并试图救醒他，但太晚了，他死了。"

"一开始，我认为这个可怜的人是在水里淹死的。但接着我看到他脖子上的黑色手指

see sb./sth. doing sth.: 看见某人/某物正在干某事

finger marks on his neck, and I knew he had been *strangled* to death! His neck was broken." When the man told us of the finger marks on the dead man's neck, I began to shake. This was the same way William had died! My blood was cold inside my body. The town leader looked at me, and then said, " You were found on the beach with a boat, and we do not know who you are. You must come with me to see the body."

Mr. Kirwin probably wanted to see what I might say or do if I saw the body. He had seen me become upset when I heard of the throat marks. So, I followed the leader to the village's inn. We went into an empty room. In the middle of the room, there was a *coffin*.

Then came the horrible moment. Even now, I cannot remember it without wanting to kill myself. I looked into the coffin to see the lifeless body.

The dead man was Henry Clerval. I threw myself on his cold dead body. I shouted and cried out, "Now three people have died because of me. How many more people will that evil monster kill, oh,

印，我知道他是被人扼死的，他的脖子都被扭断了。"当那人说到死者脖子上的黑色指印时，我开始发抖。这和威廉的死法一样！我全身发凉。市长看看我，接着说，"你被人发现乘船上岸，而且我们不认识你是谁。你必须和我一起去看那具尸体。"

科文先生可能想看看我见到尸体后会怎么说或怎么做，因为他看到我听到尸体喉头上的伤痕时很不安。因此我跟随市长到了一家乡村客栈。我们进了一间空屋，屋子中央有一副棺材。

可怕的时刻来临了，即使现在，一想起当时的情景我都想杀死我自己。我向棺材里望去，看到了那具没有生命的躯体。

死者竟是亨利·克勒瓦尔。我扑向他那冰冷的尸体。我高声哭喊："现在因为我已经死了三个人了。那个恶毒的怪物还要杀多少人呢？噢，亨利，我最好的朋友……他不该杀死你，他该杀死我！"我说不下去了。我倒在地

strangle: *v.* 勒；绞；阻碍；压抑。如：She felt her creativity was strangled. 她觉得自己的创造力被束缚了。

coffin: *n.* 棺材 [习语] a nail in sb.'s/sth.'s coffin 导致某人/某物的灭亡

Henry my best friend... He should have killed me instead! " I could not continue speaking. I fell down on the floor, unconscious.

上，失去了知觉。

CHAPTER EIGHTEEN
In Prison

For the next two months I was in prison. I *was sick with fever* and almost died. Later, when I was better, Mr. Kirwin told me that no one could understand the strange, horrible things I said in my sleep. They believed I was crazy. *Over and over* again, I cried out that I had murdered William, Henry, and Justine. I kept asking people around me to help me destroy "the monster." Often I screamed that I saw his yellow eyes watching me, and felt his fingers around my neck!

When the fever left me and I woke up, I saw that I was in a dark, dirty room. An old woman was sleeping in a chair next to my bed. "Who are you, old woman?" I asked, waking her.

"I am here to help you get well," she said loudly. "But I don't know why you would want to get well, not when you'll spend the rest of your life in prison, or worse, you killer!" I turned away

第十八章
在狱中

以后的两个月里，我被关在监狱里。我发起了高烧，几乎死去。后来，我身体好了之后，科文先生告诉我谁也不懂我梦中说的那些古怪而又可怕的事情。他们都认为我疯了。我一次又一次地哭喊是我杀了威廉、亨利和朱斯汀。我不断要求周围的人帮我除掉那个"怪物"。我经常大喊——我看见他的黄眼睛正看着我，并感到他的手指扼住了我的脖子。

等我退了烧，醒过来后，我发现自己躺在一间黑暗、肮脏的房子里。一个老妇人正在我床边的椅子上睡觉。"你是谁，老太太？"我叫醒她问道。

"我在这儿帮助你康复，"她大声说。"但我不明白你为什么还想康复，不明白当你要坐一辈子牢或者要面临更糟结局时，为什么还想康复。你这个杀人犯！"我转头不理这个凶恶的妇人。没人关心一个被认为是凶手的人。然

be sick with fever: 患热病 be
sick at/about sth./doing sth. 对
于某物/干某事使人很厌恶，很
恼火

over and over 一次又一次地

from this unkind woman. No one cared about someone they believed was a killer. However, I learned that Mr. Kirwin had sent doctors and nurses to heal me during my sickness. This was very kind, and I wondered if he thought I was a criminal. One day, when I was lying in bed, Mr. Kirwin came into my prison room. He asked, "is there anything you need? "

I looked into his eyes. They were blue and kind looking. I said, "Sir, thank you, but only death can make me happy now. I do not want to live anymore." "From the papers we found in your pocket, I learned who you are and about your family in Geneva. They are a fine family, aren't they?" I was afraid when Mr. Kirwin began to talk about my family. "No!" I cried. "Has anything happened to them? Are my father and Elizabeth all right?" "Your family is well," Mr. Kirwin told me. He smiled a little and then said, "and there is someone here to see you." I must have been very sick, because I thought that the monster had come, to tell me about how he had killed Henry. I put my

而我知道科文先生曾在我病中派医生和护士来给我看病。他这种做法真是太仁慈了，我不知道他是否也认定我是罪犯。一天，我正在床上躺着，科文先生进了我的牢房。他问我，"你需要些什么吗？"

我直视着他的眼睛。它们是蓝色的、善良的。我说，"先生，谢谢您，但现在只有死才能让我快乐，我不想活了。" "从我们在你口袋中找到的文件上，我知道了你是谁以及你在日内瓦的家庭。这是一个上等家庭，对吗？"当科文先生开始谈到我的家庭时，我非常害怕。"不！"我叫道。"他们发生了什么事吗？我父亲和伊丽莎白都好吗？" "你家里一切都安好。"科文先生对我说。他微微一笑，接着对我说，"这儿有一个人想见你。"我当时一定病得很重，因为我认为是那怪物要来告诉我他是如何杀死了亨利。我以手遮面，喊道，"不！不！不要让他进来！不要让他碰我！"显然，科文先生不知该做何想。他说，"好吧，我还认为你会想见你父亲的。"

151

hands over my eyes and shouted, "No! No! Don't let him in! Don't let him touch me!" Mr. Kirwin clearly did not know what to think. He said, "All right, but I thought that you would want to see your father."

"Wait! My father has come to see me?" I said.

"Yes, he's right here." Mr. Kirwin opened the door and my father came into the room.

I thanked God when I learned that he, Elizabeth, and my brother Ernest were all well. He did not stay long on his first visit because I was so weak. During the next month, my father was able to prove to Mr. Kirwin and the other people that I was not in Ireland at the time of Henry's death. He did this by talking to the people in the Orkney Islands, where I had been working on the monster. Immediately, the judges decided that I was not the killer, and they let me go. Now, I knew I had to return to Geneva to protect the few loved ones I had left. I had to kill the monster I had created! He had already *ruined* my life; I knew I would never be hap-

"等等！我父亲来看我了吗？"

"是的，他就在这儿。"科文先生打开门，我父亲走了进来。

当我得知父亲、伊丽莎白和我弟弟厄内斯特都安好时，我非常感激上帝的恩典。因为我身体太虚弱了，父亲第一次来探望时并没有呆多久。第二个月，我父亲已能够向科文先生和其他人证明亨利被害时我根本不在爱尔兰。他是通过和奥尼群岛的人交谈才知道这一点的，而我正是在那儿制造第二个怪物。法官们马上认定我不是凶手并立即释放了我。现在我明白我必须回日内瓦去保护我仅存的几个亲人。我必须杀死我创造的那个怪物。他已经毁了我的一生，我知道我再也不会快乐了。我知道为了父亲和伊丽莎白我必须假装高兴，但我确实感到悲惨无比。我必须杀死他，虽然我毫无力气，浑身瘦得皮包骨头。但我下定决心要回日内瓦。最终父亲同意了。在我患病期间，父亲曾听到过我说的一些梦话。但他不明白我为什么会为威廉、朱斯汀和亨利的死而自责。"我

ruin: vt. 摧毁；毁掉 *n.* 遗迹
the ruins of Pompeii 庞贝城的遗迹

py again. I would pretend I was happy for Elizabeth and my father, but I would really be miserable. But I had to kill him. My strength was gone, and my body was skin and bones. But I was so *determined* to go back to Geneva that my father finally agreed. My father had heard some of the things I had said in my sleep while I was sick. He did not understand why I blamed myself for William, Justine, and Henry's deaths. "My dear son," he told me, "You are not *responsible* for these terrible deaths. Do not say such things again. Elizabeth and I love you, and we want you to rest and get well." I wanted to kill myself at that moment, but I said nothing. My father would never know what kind of a son he had.

亲爱的儿子，你对这些人的惨死是没有责任的，不要再这样说了。我和伊丽莎白都爱你，我们想要你好好休息并尽快康复。"当时我真想杀死我自己，但我什么也没说。我父亲永远也不会知道他有一个什么样的儿子。

determined: *adj.* 有决心的；坚定的 a determined soldier 坚定的士兵 be determined to do sth. 决心干某事

responsible: *adj.* 应负责任的 be responsible for sb./sth. 对某人/某物负责任

CHAPTER NINETEEN
A Joyous Wedding

O n the day that I left Ireland I received a
letter from Elizabeth. In the letter, Elizabeth said that she still loved me, but she was not
sure how I felt. She had not spent any time with me
in many years. She had waited all these years to
marry me, but if I did not want to marry her, I did
not have to. This brave letter was not necessary. I
still loved Elizabeth, and more than anything else, I
wanted her to be my wife. But I remembered the
monster's horrible words — "I will be with you...
on the night of your marriage to sweet Elizabeth!"
I thought to myself, "If the monster wants to try
and kill me on my wedding night, all right. We will
fight until one of us is dead. If the monster wins,
I'll have peace because I'll be dead. But if I kill
him, I'll be a free man!" I was going to marry
Elizabeth, and I decided to tell her the story of the
monster after we were married. I did not want to

第十九章
欢快的婚礼

我离开爱尔兰那天，收到了伊丽莎白的一封信。在信中她说还爱着我，但不敢肯定我对她的感情如何。她已多年没和我在一起了，为嫁给我她已等了多年。但如果我不想娶她，我可以不娶。这封勇敢的信是没必要的，因为我还爱着她，比爱任何人都更强烈，我想让她作我的妻子。但我又想起了怪物那句可怕的话——"你和美丽的伊丽莎白的新婚之夜……我会到场的！"我心中想道，"如果那个怪物想在我新婚之夜杀死我，我俩将你死我活决斗到底。如果怪物取胜，我就会因死去而得到安宁。但如果我杀了他的话，我便从此自由了。"我打算娶伊丽莎白，我已决定在成婚后将怪物的事情告诉她。我不想告诉她，但她马上就要成为我的妻子。我确信，我不应该对她保密，因为我爱她。我只希望当伊丽莎白听到这种事后不会恨她的丈夫。

joyous: adj. 快乐的 a joyous sense of freedom 无忧无虑的快乐

tell her, but she was going to be my wife. I believed that I should not keep secrets from her, because I loved her. I only hoped that when Elizabeth heard the story, she would not hate her husband.

As soon as my father and I arrived in Geneva, we started to plan the wedding. When I told Elizabeth that I still loved her and wanted to marry her, she was happy. "But Victor," she said, "Do you really want to get married now? You have been so sick, and have seemed unhappy for a long time now. I can wait for you to become better." I told her that I had been sad, and that something was worrying me. "But Elizabeth, my darling, it's nothing for you to worry about, when we are so happy planning our wedding. I will tell you everything when we are married." I did not know what I would say to her, but I tried not to think about it. In the week before the wedding, I made some secret plans. I had to *get ready to* fight the monster if he attacked me. I carried a knife and a gun with me, and I was very careful when I went outside.

The wedding day was only a few days away,

我和父亲一到日内瓦，就开始筹办婚礼。当我告诉伊丽莎白我仍然爱她并愿意娶她为妻时，她非常高兴。"但是维克多，"她说，"你真的愿意现在就结婚吗？你身体一直很差，而且长期闷闷不乐。我可以等你身体好些后再结婚。"我告诉她我一直很难过，有些事一直让我烦恼。"但是亲爱的伊丽莎白，在我们幸福地筹办婚礼时，你用不着烦恼。等我们成婚后，我会把一切都告诉你。"我不知该怎样对她讲，但我尽量不去想这件事。在婚礼举办前一个星期里，我制订了一些秘密的计划。我必须做好准备——如果怪物向我攻击——我能随时投入战斗。我随身带了一把刀和一支枪，出门时也格外小心。

婚礼还有几天就要举行了。我感觉平静多

get ready to: 准备好 get ready to do sth. 准备好干某事 get ready for sth. 为某事做准备 be ready to do 正要；将要

159

and I felt calmer. I did not really believe that monster could find me on my wedding night, and I decided not to worry about it. The wedding was at our family's home. All the rooms were filled with flowers, and there were many fine ladies and gentlemen from Geneva. Elizabeth looked more beautiful than I had ever seen her. As I put a ring on her finger, I believed that my life would improve, from that moment. We decided to spend our *wedding holiday* at a house in northern Italy that had belonged to Elizabeth's family. But first, we would spend our wedding night in the town of Evian on the Lake Geneva. It was a beautiful summer day, and we were traveling across the clear blue lake in a little boat. We would spend our wedding night in a beautiful hotel in Evian. The green forests and huge mountains filled me with energy and happiness. But, as I looked at Elizabeth, I remembered that I had promised to tell Elizabeth my story when we were married. But now I was not sure I could tell her. How could I ruin her happiness? Then I felt the dark fear of the monster in my heart. He had

了，我并不真地相信那个怪物能在我的新婚之夜找到我，我决定不去为这件事烦恼。婚礼是在我家中举行的，所有的屋里都摆满了鲜花，来宾中有许多日内瓦上层社会的太太和先生们。伊丽莎白比我以前见过的任何时候都漂亮。当我给她戴上戒指时，我相信从这个时刻起，我的生活会越来越好。我们已经决定到曾经属于伊丽莎白家的、位于意大利北部的一座房子去度蜜月。但首先，我们要在日内瓦湖上的艾维安镇度过我们的新婚之夜。那是夏季的一个美丽的夜晚，我们乘一叶小舟渡过了清澈的蓝色湖泊。我们将到艾维安一家华丽的旅馆中度过我们洞房花烛夜。绿色的森林和高大的群山使我精力倍增、幸福无比。但当我看到伊丽莎白时，我想起我曾经保证过要在结婚后把我的故事都告诉伊丽莎白。不过现在我无法下决心。我怎能毁掉她的幸福呢？接着我感到了心中对怪物的恐惧，他曾说过要在我的新婚之夜找到我。

wedding holiday: 蜜月

161

said he would find me on my wedding night.

What would happen that evening? I put my hand into my pocket, where I kept a gun. I held it tightly and prayed. The sun was setting.

那个晚上会发生什么事呢？我把手伸进口袋，因为口袋里有一支手枪。我紧握住它并向天祈祷。太阳就要落山了。

CHAPTER TWENTY
The Wedding Night

I t was raining that night. Elizabeth and I watched the rain and wind from the window of our hotel room. The dark, loud storm made me afraid, because I had always seen the monster on dark, rainy nights like this. I kept touching the gun inside my pocket. Elizabeth quietly watched the *look* on my face and the fear in my eyes. Finally, she asked me, "My dear Victor, what are you afraid of? We are married now, and I am so happy."

"Don't worry, darling. It's only this storm... I don't like the weather. Once morning comes, everything will be all right," I said nervously.

I could see Elizabeth did not believe me. "Victor, what did you want to tell me? You said after we were married, you would tell me what was worrying you."

I tried hard to act normal. I said, "Really,

第二十章
新婚之夜

那天晚上天下雨了。我和伊丽莎白在旅馆的房间里望着窗外的风雨。漆黑的夜和震耳的暴雨令我害怕，因为我总是看到那个怪物在这种漆黑的雨夜里出现。我不断地伸手去摸口袋中的手枪。伊丽莎白静静地看着我脸上的神色和眼睛中的恐惧。最后，她问道，"我亲爱的维克多，你在怕什么呢？我们现在已经结婚，我非常幸福。"

"亲爱的，请别在意。只是因为这场暴雨……我不喜欢这种天气。一旦天亮，就什么事都没有了。"我紧张地说。

我看得出伊丽莎白不相信我的话。"维克多，你想对我说什么？你说过，等我们成婚后，你会告诉我是什么事情让你一直烦恼。"

我尽力表现得正常一些。我说，"真的，

look: n. 神色；神情［辨］
looks: n. 相貌。如：She inherits her father's looks. 她长相随父亲。by the look of sb. /sth. 根据某人/某物的外表

my dear, nothing is wrong. Why don't you go and lie down for a while? It has been a long day. I will be with you soon. I'm... going out for some fresh air." I had realized that if the monster and I were to meet each other that night, Elizabeth could not be there.

When I left our room, I ran through the hotel and looked outside for the monster. I looked everywhere for him, but I could not find him. I wondered if I had escaped the monster... when suddenly I heard screaming. It was coming from our room.

At that moment, I knew. I knew what the monster had really meant when he said "I will be with you on the night of your marriage." How could I have been so stupid! Crying out, I ran back to our room and opened the door — but it was too late. My wife was lying on the floor. Elizabeth was not moving, and I knew she was dead. Her mouth was opened in a scream, and her eyes had a terrible look of fear. I felt the blood leave my body, and I fell to the floor, unconscious. When I woke up, I took Elizabeth in my arms and placed

亲爱的，什么也没有。你为什么不去躺一会儿呢？已经忙了一整天啦。我很快就来陪你。我想出去透透气。"我已经意识到，如果我和那个怪物要在那天晚上会面的话，伊丽莎白是不应该在场的。

我从房中出来，跑过旅馆，到外面去寻找那个怪物。我到处搜寻，却没有找到，我想自己是否已逃出了怪物之手……突然我听到一声尖叫。尖叫是从我们的房间传出。

在那一刹那，我明白了。我明白了怪物说的"你新婚之夜我会到场的"那句话的真正含义，我怎么会这么蠢呢？我大叫一声，跑回我们的房间并打开了房门——但已经太晚了。我的妻子倒在地上。伊丽莎白一动不动，而且我知道她已经死了。她尖叫后的嘴仍然张着，眼睛里透着恐怖。我感到浑身的血似乎都流光了，随后倒在地上，失去了知觉。我苏醒过来后，双手抱起伊丽莎白，轻轻地将她放在床上。她看起来就像睡熟了似的，但脖子上留着黑色的指印。她死的方式与其他几个人一样。

her gently on the bed. She looked as if she was *asleep*, but the black finger marks were on her neck. She had died in the same way as the others.

Suddenly I heard a noise and looked up. The monster's face was in the open window, and he was staring at me. He *smiled* a horrible smile and pointed to Elizabeth's body.

" I have had my revenge, Frankenstein, my creator," he said. "Sweet Elizabeth is dead, like everyone else! I have destroyed your life, as you have destroyed mine!"

Screaming in rage, I took the gun out of my pocket and tried to shoot him, but he ran towards the lake and jumped into the water, laughing.

People had heard the sound of my gun, and they ran into the room. When they saw Elizabeth's body they cried out in horror. I told them that someone had killed her while I was out of the room. We all ran outside and looked for the killer in the woods, but after many hours we could not find the murderer. The monster was gone. I was in such pain that I could not think. I returned to my room

and sat on the bed, looking at the beautiful Elizabeth. I had not protected her from the monster, because I was too busy thinking about my own safety.
Now she was dead.

I wondered if, because the monster had hated
my father and Ernest, they were the ones I should
had failed had to return to Geneva immediately.

突然，我听到了一个声音。抬头一看，我看到怪物的脸出现在打开的窗子外面。他正盯着我，露出恶毒的笑容并指了指伊丽莎白的尸体说，

"我已经复仇了，弗兰肯斯坦，创造我的人，"他说。"美丽的伊丽莎白像其他人一样死了。就像你毁了我的一生一样，我已经把你的一生也毁了。"

我怒吼一声，从衣袋中掏出手枪并想向他开枪。但他跑到湖边，大笑着跳下了水。

人们已听到我的枪声，一起冲进了我的房间。当他们看到伊丽莎白的尸体时，吓得叫了起来。我告诉他们，有人趁我出房时杀害了她。我们一起跑出去，到树林中去搜寻那杀人犯，但数十个小时过去后，我们没有找到那个杀人犯了。怪物跑了，我痛苦得什么也想不了。我回到房间里，坐在床上，看着美丽的伊丽莎白。由于我只顾考虑自己的安全，而没能保护她免遭怪物的毒手。现在，她死了。

asleep: adj. 熟睡的（作表语）
smile: v. 笑 smile at sb./sth. 朝某人/某物笑 smile on sb./sth. 支持某人/某物

and sat on the bed, looking at the beautiful Elizabeth. I had not protected her from the monster, because I was too busy thinking about my own safety. Now, she was dead.

I wondered if the monster was going to hurt my father and Ernest. They were the only family I had left. I had to return to Geneva immediately.

我不知道那个怪物是否还会伤害我的父亲和厄内斯特。他们是我最后的亲人了。我必须马上赶回日内瓦。

CHAPTER TWENTY-ONE
The Last Fight

The news of Elizabeth's death destroyed my father. He had loved Elizabeth like a daughter, and when I told him that she was dead, he could not believe it. He could not stand the deaths of so many loved ones. A few days after my return to Geneva, my father died in his bed. The doctors told Ernest and I that it was a heart attack, but I believe he *died of* sadness. I could not stand any more pain. The deaths of William, Justine, Henry, Elizabeth, and now my father were too much for my weakened mind. I went completely mad and spent many months locked up in a hospital.

When the doctors at the hospital decided to let me go, I wanted revenge on the monster more than ever. This was my only reason for living. I wanted revenge on the monster, and I would have it. I would make him suffer for ruining my life. I would kill him. Then, I would probably *die* myself.

第二十一章
最后一战

伊丽莎白死亡的消息击倒了我父亲。他就像爱女儿一样爱着伊丽莎白。当我告诉他伊丽莎白的死讯时，他简直无法相信。所爱的人死了这么多，他实在无法承受。在我回到日内瓦几天之后，父亲就死在了床上。大夫对我和厄内斯特说父亲死于心脏病，但我相信他是死于悲哀。我无法承受更多的痛苦。对我那衰弱的大脑来讲，威廉、朱斯汀、亨利、伊丽莎白再加上现在父亲的死，对我的打击实在太大了。我完全疯了，被关在医院里住了很多月。

当医院的大夫们同意我出院时，我最想做的事就是向那个怪物复仇，而这就是我活下去的惟一原因。我要向那个怪物复仇，而且我必须复仇。因为他毁了我的生活，我必须让他吃尽苦头。我要把他杀掉，然后我也许要杀死我自己。

die of sth.: 因某事（疾病）而死

die: v. 杀死 die myself 自杀
[搭配] be dying for sth./to do sth. 渴求某物，渴求干某事

I knew I had only one choice. No one could help me find this monster, even if they believed my story. I had to find the monster myself, even if it meant spending the rest of my life doing it!

As I got ready to leave Geneva, I asked my-self, "but where should I go? That monster could be anywhere in the world now. How will I find him?" One evening a few weeks after I left the hospital, I was walking through the city. I arrived at the graveyard where William, Elizabeth, and my father were buried. I stood at their graves, and, cry-ing in pain, promised them I would make the mon-ster pay.

Suddenly I heard a soft, evil laugh. When the laughter stopped, a horrible voice I knew said, "Frankenstein, do you think you are going to make me pay? I have given you what you deserve — mis-ery! But you will live to be even more miserable. Try to find me, if you can!" I tried to find where the voice was coming from, but the monster had es-caped too quickly. *From that night on*, my last fight with the monster had begun. I had only a few clues

我知道我只有一个选择。即使有人相信我的遭遇，也没人能帮我找到那个怪物。我必须自己找到那个怪物，即使这意味着要耗尽我下半生的时光！

　　当我准备要离开日内瓦时，我问自己，"我该到哪儿去呢？现在那个怪物可能会在这个世界上的任何地方，我怎样才能找到他呢？"出院几星期后的一个晚上，我穿过城市，来到了墓地，到了埋葬威廉、伊丽莎白和我父亲的地方。我站在他们的坟前，痛苦地哭着，向他们发誓我要让那个怪物偿还血债。

　　突然我听到一阵轻轻的、恶毒的笑声。笑声刚停，一个熟悉而可怕的声音说："弗兰肯斯坦，你认为你能让我偿还血债吗？我已经给了你应得的——悲惨，但你将越来越惨。你要是有本事，就来找我吧！"我想知道声音是从哪儿发出的，但怪物逃得太快了。从那天夜里开始，我和怪物之间的最后一战开始了。我只有几条线索去寻找那个怪物，但那就足够了。几个月的时间里，我追寻他，走遍了全世界。最终，我来到了辽阔、寒冷的俄罗斯。有时，有些见过他并被他吓坏了的人告诉我他去了何

from the night on: 从那晚起

from then on：从那时起

to look for the monster, but they were enough. For many months, I followed the monster around the world. Finally, I reached the large, cold country of Russia. Sometimes, frightened people who had seen him told me where he had gone. But many times, the monster himself left clues to help me. I realized that the monster wanted me to follow him, but I did not know why. Sometimes, I found messages from him. They were lying on the ground, or placed onto rocks. Every day, I hated him more and more. I knew I would find him and kill him. While traveling north into Russia, I found his last message: "Creator, find some warm clothes and prepare for a cold, dark journey. Only your suffering will make me happy!"

I bought a sled and a group of dogs to pull the sled. With my dogs, I traveled over the snows of Russia very quickly. One night I reached a tiny village, and the people there told me a huge monster had attacked them only the night before! He had stolen their food, and tried to shoot them with guns. He had taken his own sled, and dogs. He

方。但更多时候，是怪物自己给我留下了线索。我意识到怪物想让我追逐他，但我不知道为什么。有时候我看到他留下的便条。便条或放在地上，或放在岩石上。我对他的仇恨与日俱增，我知道我要找到他并把他杀掉。北行进入俄罗斯后，我发现了他最后的一个便条："创造我的人，请找一些暖和衣服，做好准备走又冷又黑的路。只有你受苦才能让我高兴。"

我买了一架雪橇和一队拉雪橇的狗。有了狗，我在俄罗斯的雪原上跑得飞快。一天晚上，我到了一个小村子，村民们告诉我一个高大的怪物前一天晚上袭击了他们。他偷走了他们的食物并想向他们开枪。他已经坐上了自己的狗拉的雪橇，向冰封之海的方向去了。村民们对我说，"别再追他了！冰封之海极为危险。冰会在你脚下裂开，你会掉进冰下的冷水中送命的。"

went in the direction of the *frozen* sea. The villagers told me, "Don't follow him! The frozen sea is very dangerous. The ice will break under you, and you will fall into the cold water under it and die!"

But I would not listen. I had to destroy the monster!

I don't know how many weeks I spent on that ice. I had little food, and the cold was horrible. But one morning, I reached the top of an ice mountain — and saw a dark figure moving on the frozen sea below me! I could see that it was the monster. I almost cried out in joy, but I did not want him to hear me.

I followed the monster for two days, but there was still a little distance between us. However, on the third day in this area, the ice began to break and the sea began to move. I was *holding on to* a small piece of ice, watching the evil monster escape me once again! He was laughing as his sled and dogs moved away.

Soon, I could not see him any more, and I was

但我不肯听，我必须灭掉这个怪物。

　　我也不知道我在冰面上过了多少个星期。我只带了很少的食物，而且天气冷极了。但是一天早晨，我来到了一座冰山顶上——看到一个黑影正在我脚下冰封的海面上移动。我能够认出正是那怪物。我几乎兴奋地叫出声来，但我不想让他听到我的声音。

　　我追了怪物两天，但我们之间仍有一段距离。然而到了第三天，这个地区的冰层开始破裂，海水开始流动。我被困在了一小块浮冰上，眼睁睁地看着那个恶毒的怪物又一次从我身边逃走了！怪物一边赶着雪橇前行，一边哈哈大笑。

　　不久，我就再也看不见他了，我陷入了孤

freeze: *v.*冰冻〔习语〕freeze one's blood 吓得某人目瞪口呆〔辨〕frozen: 被冰冻的a frozen lake 冰封之湖 freezing: 冰冷的 freezing water冰冷的水

hold on to: 抓住 hold on: 坚持

alone. I would die a horrible death in the ice and water! I do not know how long I stayed on that piece of ice. All the dogs died. My food was gone, and I was about to give up, and throw myself into the water. Then I saw your ship. I did not know that any ships traveled in this land of ice! I broke off a piece of wood from my sled and tried to move towards your ship. Although I was weak and *about to* die, I decided not to let you help me, if your ship was going south. You see, I couldn't let anything stop me from finding the monster. But you and your men were heading north, so I let you save my life. And that is the end of my story. Although I am still weak from my travels, I will continue to look for the monster. I only hope that I live long enough.

Now, I must ask you something. Please, captain, help me. If I die before I find him, please find him and kill him for me. But don't listen to anything he says. The monster is smart, and he may try and make you feel sorry for him. Do not trust him, he is evil. Just kill him!

立无援的境地。我会惨死在冰水中！我不知道我在冰上呆了多久。所有的狗都死了，食物也吃完了。我打算放弃希望，投身于水中。接着我看到了您的船。我不知道居然还有船会在冰封的海上航行。我从雪橇上拆下一块木板奋力划向您的船。尽管我已经虚弱得快要死了，我还是决定，如果您的船向南航行，我就不接受您的帮助。您明白，我不能让任何事情阻止我找到那个怪物。但您和船员们是向北行，所以我才让你们救了我的命。这就是我故事的结尾。尽管我的身体因赶路而十分虚弱，我将继续追寻那个怪物。我只希望我能撑到那个时候。

现在，我必须求您件事。船长，请帮助我。如果我还没找到他就死了，请您找到他并替我杀死他。他说什么您都不要听。那个怪物很聪明，他可能会努力使您为他感到伤心。不要相信他的话，他是个恶人，把他杀掉就是了。

be about to 行将，将要

CHAPTER TWENTY-TWO
Peace at Last

Victor Frankenstein's story was finished. Robert Walton was amazed, but he did not know what to think of Victor Frankenstein. He was a brilliant scientist, but he had *accidentally* caused the deaths of his family. He had created a new life, but then he had left his being to suffer alone. Walton felt very sorry for Victor, but he did not really understand him. Still, he wanted to know one more thing. " Frankenstein," he asked, "please, I really want to know how, exactly, you built this creature. Tell me the secret!" "Are you crazy, Robert Walton? Haven't you listened to my story? If I tell you, you might try to create another monster, like the one that is near us now. Another horrible, evil thing! No, no one will ever know the secret. It will die with me." "But he wasn't evil at first," Walton thought to himself, but he did not say anything. He knew he could never create an-

第二十二章
最终的安宁

维克多·弗兰肯斯坦的故事讲完了。罗伯特·沃尔顿惊呆了，但他不知该如何评价维克多·弗兰肯斯坦。弗兰肯斯坦是一位杰出的科学家，但他的一念之差造成了亲人们的死亡。他创造出一个新生命，却又让他孤独受罪。沃尔顿为维克多感到悲哀，但他无法真正地理解他。他还想知道一件事。"弗兰肯斯坦，"他恳求道，"求求你，我真想知道——准确地说——你是怎样造出这个家伙的。请告诉我这个秘密。""你疯了吗，罗伯特·沃尔顿？你难道没有听我的故事吗？如果我告诉你，你可能会造出另一个怪物，就像我们身边这个家伙一样。又是一个可怕而恶毒的家伙！不，谁也别想知道这个秘密。它会随我的死去而永远消失。""但他一开始并不恶毒，"沃尔顿暗想，但他什么也没说。他知道他绝对不会创造出另一个怪物。

accidentally: *adv.* 意外地 accidental: *adj.* 意外的 an accidental meeting with a long-lost friend 邂逅一位长久不见的朋友

183

other monster.

Weeks went by, but the ship was still trapped in the ice. Walton was afraid that the ship would never be able to leave. If the ice got bigger and harder, it would destroy the ship and they would all die. Victor became weaker and weaker every day. He could not leave his bed.

Then one day, the men heard a loud cracking sound. The *solid* sea of ice was cracking, because the weather was getting warmer. The ship could move in the water. They were free! They could return to England! Everyone shouted for joy. The captain went to his room and told Victor that the ship could travel at last. "Please, don't return yet," Victor said *desperately* in a weak voice. "Help me find my enemy first." Walton said, "Frankenstein, I am sorry, but I will not put my men's lives in danger so that you can find this monster. And you are too weak to find him. Please try to understand." "Then go if you must," said Victor, "and thank you for everything you have done. But I can't go with you. I must kill the mon-

又是几个星期过去了，船仍被困在水中。沃尔顿担心船永远也走不了。如果冰越积越多，越来越硬，它就会将船挤碎，最终谁也活不成。维克多也一天比一天衰弱，已经不能下床了。

后来有一天，船员们听到一阵巨大的爆裂声。凝固的冰海正在开冻，因为天气正在变暖，船现在可以在水中移动了。他们自由了！他们可以回英格兰了！人人都在欢呼。船长到自己的舱室告诉维克多可以航行了。"求求你，别回去，"维克多用微弱的声音绝望地说，"先帮我找到我的仇敌。"沃尔顿说，"弗兰肯斯坦，我很抱歉，我不能为了让你找到那个怪物而拿我所有船员的性命去冒险。你太衰弱了，找不到他的。请您一定要理解我。""那么如果你必须走，就走吧，"维克多说，"谢谢您为我做的一切。但我不能和你们一起走，我必须杀死那个怪物。"维克多试图从床上下来，但他身体苍白、消瘦，他痛苦地叫了一声，又倒了下去，失去了知觉。等他醒过来后，几乎不能呼吸或说话。医生为维克多检查后，告诉了沃尔顿这个令人难过的消息。"先生，他只能活几个小时了。他的心脏和躯体都不行了。我无法挽救他，我很遗憾。"

solid: *n.* 固体 *adj.* 坚固的；有信誉的 a solid man 一位有诚信精神的人 **desperately:** *adv.* 孤注一掷地 desperate: *adj.* 拼命的 be desperate for sth./to do sth. 极其想得到某物，极想干某事 desperado: *n.* 亡命之徒

185

ster!" Victor tried to lift his white, thin body out
of the bed, but he cried out in pain and fell back,
unconscious. When he woke up, Victor could hard-
ly breathe or speak. When the doctor saw Victor,
he told Walton the sad news. "He has only a few
hours to live, sir. His heart and body are too sick. I
cannot help him, I'm sorry."

Robert sat in his room and stared at the *dying*
man on the bed. He was sleeping peacefully.

After some time, Victor's eyes opened, and he
whispered, "Robert, are you there? I cannot see
you. Come closer to me. I have something to say
before I die." Walton ran over and sat next to Victor.

"Walton, I do not hate the monster anymore.
All these years, a little voice in my heart told me
that I was to blame for the monster becoming angry
and terrible. I left him alone, and I should have
taught him, like a father teaches his child. But
when I finished building the monster, he was so
ugly and horrible-looking that I could not believe
what I had done. All the times I told the monster

罗伯特坐在自己的舱房内，看着床上这个垂死之人：他正安宁地睡着。

　　过了一段时间，维克多的眼睛睁开了。他低声道，"罗伯特，你在这儿吗？我看不见你。靠近一点。我死前有话要说。"沃尔顿上前坐在了维克多旁边。

　　"沃尔顿，我不再恨那个怪物了。这些年中，我心中总有一个轻微的声音对我说——在使怪物变得愤怒和凶恶这件事上我应受到责备。我把他独自扔下，而我本应教导他，就像一个父亲教导孩子那样。但我造出这个怪物后，他太丑陋、太凶恶了，使我对我所做的一切感到难以置信。我一直对那个怪物说我恨他以及我有多么怕他——沃尔顿，我其实是怕我自己。我才是真正的怪物，而不是他。"

dying: adj. 临死的；弥留之际的

that I hated him, and how I was afraid of him — Walton, I was really afraid of myself. I was the real monster, not him."

" He might have had a good life if I had helped him. But now, it is too late. He hates people now, and he must be stopped before he kills anyone else. Please... if you see him, kill him. Do not kill him because he is ugly, or because he has killed people. Kill him because then he will also have peace."

Then Frankenstein said something amazing. "Monster... if you are watching me, I forgive you for killing my family. And, I am sorry. " With that, Victor held the hand of his last friend on earth. His mouth formed a soft, gentle smile and his eyes closed forever.

That night Walton was standing on the ship's deck looking at the beautiful moon and stars. He was thinking about Victor. Suddenly, he heard a strange voice. It was coming from the room where Victor's body lay. Walton knew what was happening. He ran to the room and saw a large *shape*

"如果我肯帮助他的话，他可能会过上好日子的。但现在，一切都太晚了。他现在痛恨人类，必须在他杀死其他人以前阻止他。求你——如果你见到他，把他杀掉。不是因为他丑陋而杀死他，或因为他杀了人而杀死他。杀死他是因为他死后就会获得安宁。"

接着弗兰肯斯坦说了些令人吃惊的话："怪物……如果你正在看着我，你听着，我饶恕了你杀死我亲人的恶行。而且，我很抱歉。"说了这句话，维克多握住了他在人世间最后一位朋友的手。他的嘴角浮现出一个温柔、和蔼的微笑，然后就永远地闭上了双眼。

那天晚上，沃尔顿站在船的甲板上望着美丽的月亮和星星。他在想着维克多。突然，他听到从停放维克多尸体的舱房里传出一个奇怪的声音。他看到一个巨大的身躯站在维克多的尸体旁。怪物正抓着维克多那冰冷的手哭泣，那种声音连沃尔顿听了都感到难受。怪物发现到沃尔顿正看着他时，跳起来跑向窗户。　"等

shape: *n.* 形状；身材；身影
give shape to sth. 清晰地表达
shapely: *adj.* 身材好的

189

standing by Victor's body. The monster was crying as he held Victor's cold hand. The sound was painful for Walton to listen to. When he saw Walton watching him, the monster jumped up and ran towards the window. "Wait! Stay! I know who you are!" said the captain.

The monster pointed down at Victor and said, "He is my last victim. I will never kill again. Oh, I only wish he could forgive me for destroying all the people he loved!" At first, Walton wanted to follow Victor's last wish and kill the monster. He was ugly, and miserable. He could never be happy on this earth. But, somehow, Walton did not think he could do that. He said, "Monster, I wish you had never done these terrible things. Frankenstein was wrong to treat you so cruelly, but why did you kill innocent people? They did not *deserve* to die! Victor died alone, with no one to love him. What do you say to that?" "I have many things to say, human. I hated the things I did. I thought only of my own pain and anger. I only wanted to make Frankenstein as unhappy as I was. But I was not al-

一下! 站住! 我知道你是谁!"船长喊道。

　　怪物向下指着维克多说，"他是我最后的牺牲品。我不会再杀人了。噢，我只是希望他能够饶恕我杀死了所有他爱的人!"一开始，沃尔顿想了却维克多最后一个心愿，把这个怪物杀掉。他既丑陋、又悲惨，在这个世界上永远也不会幸福的。但不知怎么，沃尔顿认为他不能那样做。他说，"怪物，我真希望你没有做过这许多恶行。弗兰肯斯坦如此残忍地对待你固然不对，但你为什么要杀死无辜的人呢?他们可不该死! 维克多孤独地死去了，没有人去爱他。对此你怎么说?" "我有许多话要说，人啊。我痛恨我所做的那些事，我只想到了我一个人的痛苦和愤怒。我只想让弗兰肯斯坦变得和我一样难过。但我并非一直是这个样子的。我的生命刚开始时，我也是一个善良的、充满爱心的人。我对弗兰肯斯坦和其他人所要求的只是关心我、看到我内在的优点而已。但他们痛恨我、害怕我，仅仅因为我是异类。没有人肯给我一个机会。这一切改变了我。有时我也为弗兰肯斯坦感到遗憾。我曾经杀死了他

deserve: *v.* 值得。如：The pupil deserved to be praised. 这个学生值得表扬。

191

ways this way. I began my life as a good, *loving* being. All I wanted was for Frankenstein, and other people, to care about me, and see the goodness inside me. But no one did that. They only hated and feared me because I am different. No one gave me a chance. That is what changed me. " Sometimes I was sorry for Frankenstein, I had killed his little brother, and then another person, the servant girl, died because of what I did. But then Frankenstein broke his promise to make me a friend. And I learned Frankenstein was going to marry, and have a happy life for himself while I was alone. Then, my feelings of sorrow turned to hatred. I killed his best friend, and then his wife. How sorry I am now." Robert remembered what Victor had said. "He will try to make you feel sorry for him." Suddenly he was angry at the horrible-looking thing, and said, 'Monster, you ruined Frankenstein's life, and he died, sick and almost crazy, because of you. Now, you come here asking his forgiveness? The only thing you know now is hatred!"

The monster's sad yellow eyes looked at Wal-

的弟弟；然后，另一个人——那个侍女也因为我的行动而死。但后来弗兰肯斯坦违背了他的诺言，不肯给我造出一个朋友。我得知弗兰肯斯坦要结婚了，他自己要过快乐的生活而让我孤苦伶仃。那时，我的悲哀变成了仇恨。我杀死了他最好的朋友，然后是他的妻子。我现在是多么后悔啊！"罗伯特想起了维克多说过的话，"他会想法儿让你为他感到伤心的。"罗伯特突然对这个长相凶恶的东西感到愤怒，说道："怪物，你毁了弗兰肯斯坦的一生，而且就因为你，他重病缠身，几乎神智失常地死去了。现在，你到这儿来还想请求他的饶恕吗？你现在所知道的一切就是仇恨。"

怪物那双悲哀的黄眼睛看着沃尔顿。"你

loving: adj. 富含爱意的 loving words 充满爱的话语

ton. "What do you know about hate? Why don't you hate Felix, who attacked me and drove me away, when I was becoming friends with his old, blind father? Why don't you hate the man who shot me after I saved his little girl's life? I have been beaten, hated, feared, and left alone by humans. Why shouldn't I hate them? Now that you have seen me, you hate and fear me too... but not as much as I hate myself. But do not be frightened. The only murder I will commit now is my own. I will leave your ship and travel to a quiet, lonely spot. There, where no one can find me, I will build a fire and burn my miserable body to ashes. Then the wind will take those ashes into the sea. In this way, no part of my body will be found. I do not want a curious person to try to create another being like me. No one should ever have to feel the pain I have felt! So now I will say, 'Goodbye, human. Goodbye, Victor Frankenstein. If you are watching me, you should know that I am sorry now. Good-bye!'"

And the monster jumped through the window.

Robert ran towards the window after him, cry-

知道什么叫做仇恨吗？你为什么不去恨费利克斯，当我就要成为他那盲父的朋友时，他却袭击我并将我赶走！你为什么不去恨那个我救了他女儿性命，反而开枪打我的那个人？我被人类殴打、痛恨、害怕，而且孤苦伶仃。我为什么不该恨他们？既然你见到了我，你也对我又恨又怕，可哪比得上我对自己的仇恨？不过别害怕，我现在要杀的惟——个人就是我自己。我要离开你的船到一个安静的、无人知道的地方。在哪儿，谁也找不到我，我要生起一堆火并把我这悲惨的身躯烧成灰烬。然后风会把我的骨灰吹进大海。这样，谁也不会找到我身体的任何一部分。我不想让一个好奇的人再造出一个像我这样的人。谁也不用再遭受我曾遭受过的痛苦了！所以现在，我要说，'再见了，人类。再见了，维克多·弗兰肯斯坦。如果你在看着我，你会知道我现在已经后悔了。再见了！'"

接着，怪物穿窗而出。

罗伯特紧跟着追向窗户，喊道，"等等！

ing, "Wait! I have something to tell you..." but the monster was not listening. Walton had wanted to tell the monster that Frankenstein had understood and forgiven him, before he died. But it was too late. The monster was already on a raft, traveling quickly over the water. He was crying loudly. In moments, the monster was far away, lost in the darkness.

我有话要对你说……"但怪物却不听。沃尔顿想告诉怪物弗兰肯斯坦临死前已经理解并宽恕了他。但一切都太晚了,怪物已跳上了一只木筏,飞快地在水面上前行。他放声大哭。很快,怪物远去了,消失在了黑暗之中。

床头灯英语学习读本

Ⅰ.《查泰莱夫人的情人》　　　　《彼得·潘》

《飘》　　　　　　　　　　　《格列佛游记》

《红与黑》　　　　　　　　　《黑骏马》

《了不起的盖茨比》　　　　　《汤姆·索亚历险记》

《歌剧魅影》　　　　　　　　《杨柳风》

《三个火枪手》　　　Ⅲ.《德伯家的苔丝》

《傲慢与偏见》　　　　　　　《化身博士》

《呼啸山庄》　　　　　　　　《野性的呼唤》

《简·爱》　　　　　　　　　《阿丽思漫游奇境记》

《儿子与情人》　　　　　　　《弗兰肯斯坦》

Ⅱ.《鲁滨逊漂流记》　　　　　　《白鲸》

《大战火星人》　　　　　　　《环游地球 80 天》

《巴斯克维尔猎犬》　　　　　《圣诞欢歌》

《时间机器》　　　　　　　　《圣经故事》

《远大前程》　　　　　　　　《希腊神话故事》

考试虫丛书学术委员会

推 荐 书 目

书名　介绍	版　别	定价
考试虫系列－大学英语四、六级考试		
大学英语四级考试 辅导讲义 　四级考试一本通。	航空工业	25.00
大学英语四级考试 辅导讲义(音带2盒)	开明文教	14.00
英语词汇速听速记手册—1－4级词汇掌中宝	航空工业	8.00
(盒装)英语词汇速听速记手册—1－4级词汇掌中宝 (1书3带)	开明文教	29.00
英语词汇速听速记手册—1－6级词汇掌中宝	航空工业	8.00
(盒装)英语词汇速听速记手册—1－6级词汇掌中宝 (1书4带)	开明文教	36.00
磨耳朵——大学英语四级词汇(书1本音带5盒)	开明文教	36.00
磨耳朵——大学英语六级词汇(书1本音带2盒)	开明文教	17.00
大学英语1－4级词汇手边书(新) 　书不大,信息含量高,建议同学们将此书读16～ 25遍。	航空工业	12.80
大学英语5－6级词汇手边书(新)	航空工业	8.80
大学英语四级词汇串讲 　详略得当,快速串讲。	航空工业	15.00
大学英语六级词汇串讲	航空工业	19.00
大学英语1～4级词汇记忆考点札记 　记忆＋考点	航空工业	25.00
大学英语5～6级词汇记忆考点札记	航空工业	13.00

书名　介绍	版　别	定价
大学英语四级考试四会式词汇	航空工业	13.00
大学英语四级词汇"考试虫"记忆树	航空工业	15.00
大学英语六级词汇"考试虫"记忆树	航空工业	16.00
大学英语四级考试 听力高分有术 　　听力技巧专著,是听力应试最高境界的体现。	航空工业	10.00
大学英语四级考试 听力高分有术(音带3盒)	开明文教	21.00
大学英语六级考试 听力高分有术	航空工业	10.00
大学英语六级考试 听力高分有术(音带3盒)	开明文教	21.00
大学英语四、六级考试 听力高分有术	航空工业	17.00
大学英语四、六级考试 听力高分有术(音带4盒)	开明文教	28.00
大学英语四、六级考试 听力高分有术(精华版) **(书1本,音带2盒)** 　　精选了《大学英语四、六级考试听力高分有术》书中部分精华内容,并配2盒音带。	开明文教	20.00
大学英语四、六级考试 万能作文 　　本书采用万能写作模式,使考生能在最短时间内提高自己的英语写作水平。	航空工业	12.00
大学英语四、六级考试 万能作文(背诵版) 　　精选了《大学英语四、六级考试万能作文》中范文,并配上录音,使你可以闭着眼睛背作文。	开明文教	8.00
大学英语阅读基本功——难句过关 　　如果把难句都掰扯明白了,那阅读不就过关了嘛!	航空工业	12.00
大学英语阅读基本功——难句过关(1书3带)	北京电视 艺术中心	33.00
大学英语四级考试 阅读手记 　　阅读技巧专著,被誉为"四级阅读冲刺第一书"。	航空工业	18.00

书名 介绍	版 别	定价
大学英语六级考试 阅读手记	航空工业	22.00
大学英语语法考点手册 　　专门把四级语法考点提炼出来，重点突出，针对性强。适合四级考试有 40 或 50 分实力的人使用。	航空工业	12.00
最新大学英语语法考点	航空工业	12.00
大学英语四级考试 听力模拟题与精听训练 （书 1 本，音带 3 盒） 　　八套题，清华大学黄淑琳教授主编	开明文教	26.00
大学英语四级考试"考试虫"试卷	航空工业	12.00
大学英语四级考试 "考试虫"试卷(音带 3 盒)	开明文教	21.00
大学英语六级考试"考试虫"试卷	航空工业	12.00
大学英语六级考试 "考试虫"试卷(音带 3 盒)	开明文教	21.00
大学英语四级考试冲刺试卷(其中 8 套试题 7.00 元)	航空工业	12.00
大学英语四级考试冲刺试卷(音带 2 盒)	开明文教	14.00
大学英语四级考试全题型模拟题精解(二)(其中 10 套试卷 8.00 元，教案 14.80 元) 　　十套题，解答详尽。	航空工业	22.80
大学英语四级考试全题型模拟题精解(二)(音带 3 盒)	开明文教	21.00
大学英语四级考试优化训练试卷 　　本书试题的命制经命题、初审、预测、试卷项目分析、审题和构卷等多个流程完成，具有很高的信度、效度和很强的科学性。	航空工业	15.00
大学英语四级考试优化训练试卷(音带 3 盒)	开明文教	21.00

书名　介绍	版　别	定价
最新大学英语考试题库精解(四级)(其中 10 套试卷 10.00 元) 　　十套题,试题活页分装,解答详尽。可方便教师备课。	航空工业	29.00
最新大学英语考试题库精解(四级)(音带 3 盒)	开明文教	21.00
洞穿四级——大学英语四级考试历年实考试题解析 　　最新 10 套全真题、全译本	航空工业	13.80
洞穿四级——大学英语四级考试历年实考试题解析 (音带 3 盒)	开明文教	21.00
洞穿六级——大学英语六级考试历年实考试题解析 　　最新 10 套全真题、全译本	航空工业	13.80
洞穿六级——大学英语六级考试历年实考试题解析 (音带 3 盒)	开明文教	21.00
大学英语历年实考试题解析(四级) 　　最新 15 套(合适的考前训练量)全真题及精解,如果把 15 套全真题都弄懂,那四级也就过关了。	航空工业	20.00
大学英语历年实考试题解析(四级)(音带 4 盒)	开明文教	28.00
大学英语历年实考试题解析(六级) 　　最新 15 套(合适的考前训练量)全真题及精解,如果把 15 套全真题都弄懂,那六级也就过关了。	航空工业	20.00
大学英语历年实考试题解析(六级)(音带 4 盒)	开明文教	28.00
考试虫系列－考研:		
英语词汇速听速记手册—考研词汇掌中宝	航空工业	8.00
(盒装)英语词汇速听速记手册—考研词汇掌中宝(1 书 4 带) 　　所有英文词条都有录音、标准美音、中央台合成。	开明文教	36.00

书名　介绍	版　别	定价
磨耳朵——考研英语听力词汇(1书4带) 　　所有英文词条和例句都有录音,建议听16~25遍,打通耳关。	北京电视 艺术中心	36.00
硕士研究生入学考试英语四会式词汇	航空工业	15.00
硕士研究生入学考试英语词汇"考试虫"记忆树	航空工业	20.00
MBA联考英语词汇掌中宝	北京电视 艺术中心	8.00
MBA联考英语词汇掌中宝(音带4盒)	北京电视 艺术中心	28.00
MBA联考英语词汇掌中宝(1书4带)	北京电视 艺术中心	36.00
工商管理硕士入学考试MBA万能作文(英语) 　　单句写作与篇章写作相结合;万能模式写作与自由写作相结合;两周背下万能模板,胜过考前苦读百篇作文。	航空工业	20.00
硕士研究生入学考试 英语听力模拟题与精听训练(书1本,音带3盒) 　　清华大学黄淑琳教授精心命制的8套考研听力模拟题与精听训练。	开明文教	26.00
硕士研究生入学考试 英语辅导讲义 　　本书融合了北大毕金献教授对考研命题的深刻理解和"考试虫"总主编王若平博士对英语考试的切身体会及"考试虫"学习体系教授团队呕心沥血的工作而成。	航空工业	42.00
硕士研究生入学考试 英语辅导讲义(音带2盒)	开明文教	14.00
考研英语听力基本功——听写训练①~④(书1本,音带2盒) 　　听写训练是提高听力的必由之路。如果您真想提高听力,就静下心来,踏踏实实地练习听写。	开明文教	17.00

书名 介绍	版 别	定价
硕士研究生英语入学考试 阅读基本功(难句过关) 如果把难句都掰扯明白了,那阅读不就过关了嘛!	航空工业	20.00
硕士研究生英语入学考试 阅读基本功(难句过关)(1书3带)	北京电视 艺术中心	41.00
硕士研究生英语入学考试 阅读手记 阅读技巧专著,被誉为"考研阅读冲刺第一书"。	航空工业	25.00
硕士研究生英语入学考试 万能作文 采用万能模式,使考生能在最短时间内提高自己的考试写作水平。"两周背下万能模式,胜过考前苦读百篇作文。"	航空工业	20.00
硕士研究生英语入学考试 万能作文(背诵版) 精选了《硕士研究生英语入学考试万能作文》中范文,并配上录音,使你可以闭着眼睛背作文。	开明文教	10.00
洞穿考研——硕士研究生英语入学考试历年实考试题解析 帮助考生从历年实考试题中吸取精华;答题的最高境界是再现。	航空工业	39.00
洞穿考研——硕士研究生英语入学考试历年实考试题解析(音带2盒)	开明文教	14.00
硕士研究生英语入学考试 词汇记忆考点札记 本书编写历时两载,浓缩:记忆＋考点。	航空工业	17.00
洞穿考研数学(理工类) 最贴近考生需求的考研数学书,实用性强。	航空工业	44.00
洞穿考研数学(经济类)	航空工业	39.00
硕士研究生入学考试 陈先奎政治8套模拟试卷 山不在高,有仙则名;题不在多,有陈先奎押题则灵。	航空工业	13.00

书名　介绍	版　别	定价
陈先奎政治考前串讲讲义 　　听过陈先奎课的人都领教过他串讲和押题功夫，您该试试。	航空工业	20.00
硕士研究生入学考试"考试虫"英语 8 套模拟试卷 　　主编：毕金献(原教育部考研英语命题组组长)，王若平："考试虫"	航空工业	13.00
硕士研究生入学考试"考试虫"数学(数 1、2、3、4)8 套模拟试卷 　　主编：原教育部考研数学资深命题人员：范培华教授(1987—2000 年命题)，李恒沛教授(1987—2001年命题)，胡金德教授(1989—1997 年命题)，王式安教授(1987—2001 年命题)，周概容教授(1987—2003 年命题)。可以说，他们对考研数学命题绝对有最深刻、最权威的把握。	航空工业	10.00 (估)/册
硕士研究生政治入学考试哲学、政经重难点分析 　　最难啃的骨头要先啃	航空工业	15.00
硕士研究生政治入学考试政治辅导讲义	航空工业	40.00
硕士研究生政治入学考试政治核心试题	航空工业	30.00
硕士研究生政治入学考试形势与政策及核心试题增编	航空工业	15.00
硕士研究生政治入学考试政治考前 50 题	航空工业	12.00
同等学力人员申请硕士学位英语统考应试指南(修订三版) 　　本书作者对同等学力人员申请硕士学位英语统考有深入研究，此书是一本金牌书。	航空工业	34.00
同等学力人员申请硕士学位英语统考应试指南 (音带 4 盒)	开明文教	28.00
同等学力人员申请硕士学位英语水平全国统一考试专家点评	航空工业	16.80
同等学力人员申请硕士学位英语水平全国统一考试专家点评(音带 3 盒)	开明文教	21.00

书名　介绍	版　别	定价
考试虫系列－自学考试：		
自考词汇掌中宝 　　先听、再说、后写是人类学习语言的本能，是记忆单词、增强语感最朴实的方法。	开明文教	8.00
自考词汇掌中宝(音带4盒) 　　所有英文词条都配有录音、标准美音、中央台合成。	开明文教	28.00
(盒装)自考词汇掌中宝(1书4带)	开明文教	36.00
美国播音员教你读课文 　　美国播音员教你读《大学英语自学教程》上册A篇生词及课文　慢速	北京电视艺术中心	25.00
考试虫系列－大学英语学习与考试：		
大学新生入学英语衔接丛书——听力① 　　试题12套，难度：一级，选材新，趣味性强，解答详尽。	开明文教	10.00
大学新生入学英语衔接丛书——听力①(音带4盒) 　　录音语速较慢，语音标准（美音）、清楚，中央台合成。	开明文教	28.00
大学新生入学英语衔接丛书——听力② 　　试题12套，难度：二级，选材新，趣味性强，解答详尽。	开明文教	10.00
大学新生入学英语衔接丛书——听力②(音带4盒) 　　录音语速较慢，语音标准（美音）、清楚，中央台合成。	开明文教	28.00
大学新生入学英语衔接丛书——阅读① 　　80篇文章，每篇文章均按四级考试阅读模式出题，难度一级，选材好，趣味性强，解答详尽。	航空工业	15.00
大学新生入学英语衔接丛书——阅读② 　　80篇文章，每篇文章均按四级考试阅读模式出题，难度二级，选材好，趣味性强，解答详尽。	航空工业	15.00

书名　介绍	版　别	定价
英语词汇速听速记手册——《新编大学英语》词汇掌中宝 　　是《新编大学英语》教材的词汇本。	开明文教	8.00
英语词汇速听速记手册——《新编大学英语》词汇掌中宝(音带4盒) 　　所有英文词条都配有录音、标准美音、中央台合成。	开明文教	28.00
英语词汇速听速记手册——《大学英语·精读》 **(1-4册)词汇掌中宝** 　　是《大学英语·精读》教材的词汇本。	开明文教	4.00
英语词汇速听速记手册——《大学英语·精读》 **(1-4册)词汇掌中宝**(音带2盒)	开明文教	14.00
《大学英语·精读》词汇记忆考点札记 　　记忆+考点	航空工业	18.00
钻研《大学英语·精读》①～④ 　　本书对《大学英语·精读》课文逐字逐句进行精炼讲解,使您轻松彻底弄懂课文。	航空工业	12.00/册
英语词汇速听速记手册——《新概念英语》(1-4册) **词汇掌中宝** 　　《新概念英语》教材的词汇本。	航空工业	4.00
英语词汇速听速记手册——《新概念英语》(1-4册) **词汇掌中宝**(音带2盒)	开明文教	14.00
钻研《新概念英语》①～④ 　　谨以此书献给那些英语学了多年,却没有入门的同学;那些在中高级英语考试中屡战屡败,屡败屡战并试图通过英语来改变自身命运的人;那些曾经学过英语,但已丢了多年,想重新开始学英语的人。	航空工业	23.00/册

书名　介绍	版　别	定价
《新编大学英语》①～③示范教案	航空工业	15.00/册
《新编大学英语》④示范教案	航空工业	17.00
《新编大学英语》①～④词汇记忆考点札记	航空工业	12.00/册
教你学《21世纪大学英语·读写教程》①～④	航空工业	12.00/册
大学英语循序渐进听力训练1(书1本,音带3盒) 　　本书是以"听力不可能速成"为指导思想,根据大学英语教学和考试大纲编写的一套循序渐进的英语精听教材。一级:句子填空,单句听辨,对话听辨等。	开明文教	26.00
大学英语循序渐进听力训练2(书1本,音带3盒) 　　二级:句子听写,对话听辨,段落听辨等。	开明文教	26.00
大学英语循序渐进听力训练3(书1本,音带3盒) 　　三级:句子及复合听写,对话听辨(十大主题),段落听辨等。	开明文教	26.00
大学英语循序渐进听力训练4(书1本,音带3盒) 　　四级:对话听辨,复合听写,段落听辨(标准四级考试题型)。	开明文教	26.00
大学英语三级听力全题型训练 　　试题12套,难度:大英三级,选材新,趣味性强,解答详尽,录音语速较慢,语音标准(美音)、清楚,中央台合成。	航空工业	12.00
大学英语三级听力全题型训练(音带4盒)	北京电视艺术中心	28.00
英语词汇速听速记手册——常用口语词汇掌中宝	开明文教	4.00
英语词汇速听速记手册——常用口语词汇掌中宝(音带2盒)	开明文教	14.00

书名　介绍	版　别	定价
(盒装)英语词汇速听速记手册——常用口语词汇掌中宝(1书2带)	开明文教	18.00
大学英语词汇讲座和练习 　　本书最大的特点是滴水不漏，覆盖了四、六级考试词汇的所有测试点。如果你把这本书读透了，词汇题就没有不会做的。	航空工业	18.00
大学英语语法讲座和练习(修订五版) 　　语法是成年人学英语的捷径。本书对英语的语法进行了全面讲解，其练习设计得尤为实用。	航空工业	21.00
大学英语写作讲座和练习(修订三版)	兵器工业	8.50
洞穿雅思—雅思考试真题分析与实练 　　最贴近考生需求，实用性强。	航空工业	20.00
床头灯英语学习读本Ⅰ： 　　三千词读遍天下书。 　　喜欢读有趣的故事、小说是人类的天性。这套读物使得你不用翻字典，躺在床上就可以津津有味地学英语，把长期的、艰苦的英语学习变成一件有意思的事情，不需要很强的自制力，就能把英语学习坚持下来。		
查泰莱夫人的情人	航空工业	10.00
飘	航空工业	10.00
红与黑	航空工业	10.00
了不起的盖茨比	航空工业	10.00
歌剧魅影	航空工业	10.00
三个火枪手	航空工业	10.00
傲慢与偏见	航空工业	10.00

书名　介绍	版　别	定价
呼啸山庄	航空工业	10.00
简·爱	航空工业	10.00
儿子与情人	航空工业	10.00
床头灯英语学习读本Ⅱ：		
鲁滨逊漂流记	航空工业	10.00
大战火星人	航空工业	10.00
巴斯克维尔猎犬	航空工业	10.00
时间机器	航空工业	10.00
远大前程	航空工业	10.00
彼得·潘	航空工业	10.00
格列佛游记	航空工业	10.00
黑骏马	航空工业	10.00
汤姆·索亚历险记	航空工业	10.00
杨柳风	航空工业	10.00
床头灯英语学习读本Ⅲ：		
吸血鬼	航空工业	10.00
化身博士	航空工业	10.00
野性的呼唤	航空工业	10.00
阿丽思漫游奇境记	航空工业	10.00
弗兰肯斯坦	航空工业	10.00
白鲸	航空工业	10.00

书名　介绍	版　别	定价
环游地球 80 天	航空工业	10.00
圣诞颂歌	航空工业	10.00
圣经故事	航空工业	10.00
希腊神话故事	航空工业	10.00
有声读物系列:		
猫咪凯蒂和小老鼠(音带版)(1 书 1 音带)	开明文教	15.00
猫咪凯蒂和小老鼠(CD 版)(1 书 1CD)	开明文教	16.00
兔山(音带版)(1 书 1 音带)	开明文教	15.00
兔山(CD 版)(1 书 1CD)	开明文教	16.00
爸爸和我(音带版)(1 书 1 音带)	开明文教	15.00
爸爸和我(CD 版)(1 书 1CD)	开明文教	16.00
又来了一只狗(音带版)(1 书 1 音带)	开明文教	15.00
又来了一只狗(CD 版)(1 书 1CD)	开明文教	16.00
动物和数字(音带版)(1 书 1 音带)	开明文教	15.00
动物和数字(CD 版)(1 书 1CD)	开明文教	16.00
考试虫英语美文选(书 1 本,音带 4 盒) 选文精,译文水平一流,美籍演员朗诵。	开明文教	36.00
正音——美语发音基本功(书 1 本,音带 2 盒) 一针见血地指出了中国人说英语的习惯性错误,采用针对中国人的矫治训练。中式发音→美式发音。	航空工业	24.00
正音——美语发音基本功	航空工业	10.00
正音——美语发音基本功(音带 2 盒)	开明文教	14.00

书名　介绍	版　别	定价
English Small Talk(英语小对话)(书1本,音带2盒) 　　由美国教育家丹尼斯夫妇为中国人写的口语书,语音地道、优美,是美国人现在讲的英语。由美国播音员和演员在美国录制。	开明文教	22.00/套
标准美国英语口语(音带版)(1书4带)	开明文教	32.00
标准美国英语口语(CD版)(1书4CD)	开明文教	36.00
英语听力基本功——听写训练①(书1本,音带2盒) 　　泰坦尼克号故事,语音纯正,优美,听起来是种享受。听写训练是提高听力的必由之路。本书是听力基础薄弱的同学之必读书。	开明文教	18.00
英语听力基本功——听写训练②(书1本,音带2盒) 　　THE BIG SPLASH故事,语音纯正,优美,听起来是种享受。	开明文教	18.00
国句名篇(书1本、CD、VCD各1张)(北京大学许渊冲教授汉诗英译精选) 　　翻译家许渊冲先生汉诗英译53首,精制成一张CD;英文朗诵:Kristopher Chung;中文朗诵,林如(中央人民广播电台资深播音员),配乐:宋铁铮(中央台资深配乐);中央台节目东方之子——翻译家许渊冲(赠一张VCD)。	开明文教	22.00/套
最好的儿童英文歌曲(一)(书1本,音带2盒) 　　由美国教育家丹尼斯夫妇合编,音带中有原唱歌曲和丹尼斯朗诵的英文歌词,中央台合成。	开明文教	22.00/套
最好的儿童英文歌曲(二)(书1本,音带2盒)	开明文教	22.00/套
最好的英文歌谣(书1本,音带2盒,彩印) 　　丹尼斯夫妇在美国花了近两年的时间收集编写的英文歌谣,由美国演员录音。从中不但可以学到地道的英文,而且可以了解英美文化。	开明文教	26.00/套

书名　介绍	版　别	定价
英文金曲赏析(精华版)(书1本,音带2盒) 　　中英文歌词与赏析、语言难点注释。音带里包含英文歌词朗诵和原声金曲,中央台合成。	开明文教	22.00/套
英文金曲赏析(一)～(九) (书1本,音带2盒) 　　有位专家说,如果把这200首曲听透,那英文水平肯定会提高。	开明文教	22.00/辑
英文背诵圣典(一)～(五) (书1本,音带2盒) 　　小说、散文、电影、诗歌、演讲等名段及实用写作;音带:书中名篇的朗诵以及名曲配乐。	开明文教	18.00/辑
大学英语之声——《大学英语》2001年精华版(书1本,音带2盒)	开明文教	20.00
大学英语之声——《大学英语》2002年精华版(书1本,音带3盒)	北京电视艺术中心	26.00
考试虫英文电影课堂:		
音乐之声(音带版)(1书2带)	开明文教	22.00
音乐之声(CD版)(1书2CD)	开明文教	24.00
罗马假日(音带版)(1书2带)	开明文教	22.00
罗马假日(CD版)(1书2CD)	开明文教	24.00
简·爱(音带版)(1书2带)	开明文教	22.00
简·爱(CD版)(1书2CD)	开明文教	24.00
人鬼情未了(音带版)(1书2带)	开明文教	22.00
人鬼情未了(CD版)(1书2CD)	开明文教	24.00
魂断蓝桥(音带版)(1书2带)	开明文教	22.00

书名　介绍	版　别	定价
魂断蓝桥(CD版)(1书2CD)	开明文教	24.00
飘(音带版)(1书2带)	开明文教	22.00
飘(CD版)(1书2CD)	开明文教	24.00
爱情故事(音带版)(1书2带)	开明文教	22.00
爱情故事(CD版)(1书2CD)	开明文教	24.00
泰坦尼克号(音带版)(1书2带)	开明文教	22.00
泰坦尼克号(CD版)(1书2CD)	开明文教	24.00
阿甘正传(音带版)(1书2带)	开明文教	22.00
阿甘正传(CD版)(1书2CD)	开明文教	24.00
狮子王(音带版)(1书2带)	开明文教	22.00
狮子王(CD版)(1书2CD) 　　通过英文原版电影学英语无疑是学英语的最好方法,但很多人弄不懂电影对白,本系列讲解部分不放过任何一个疑难之处,帮你彻底看懂电影。	开明文教	24.00

全国各大外文、新华、民营书店均有售。

销售咨询电话: 010-82863352　82867367　84841802

北京零售地址: 海淀西大街 36 号海淀图书城昊海楼 108 英汉达书店

电话: 62534432

北京学考圆书店(北航北门斜对面)

电话:82381301

北京市海淀区学院路 9 号 109、228-230 号

电话: 82370959(60)　82370956